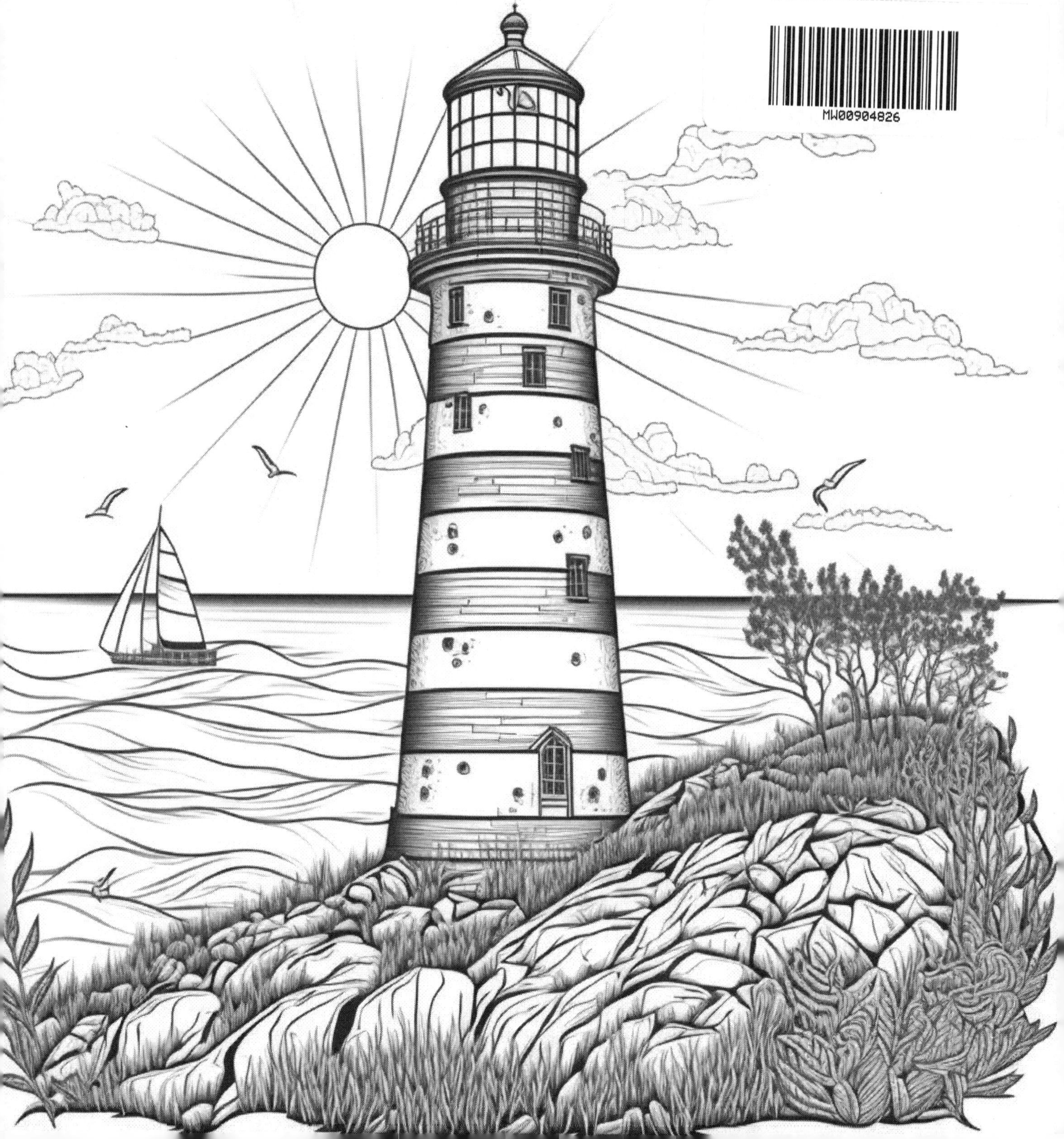

Totally Coastal

Adult Coloring Book

This book belongs to:

____

Designed by Brandon Razinha

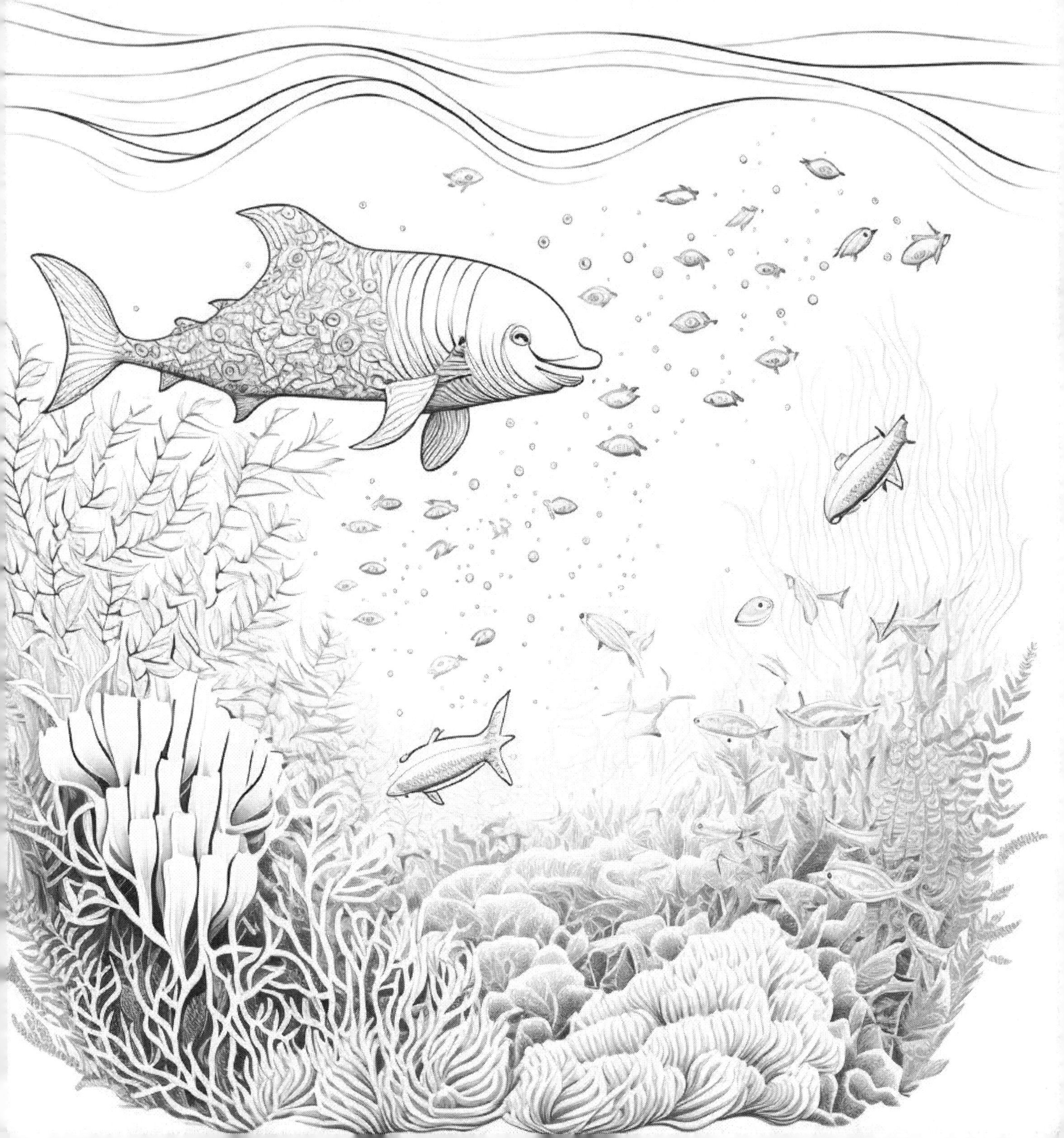

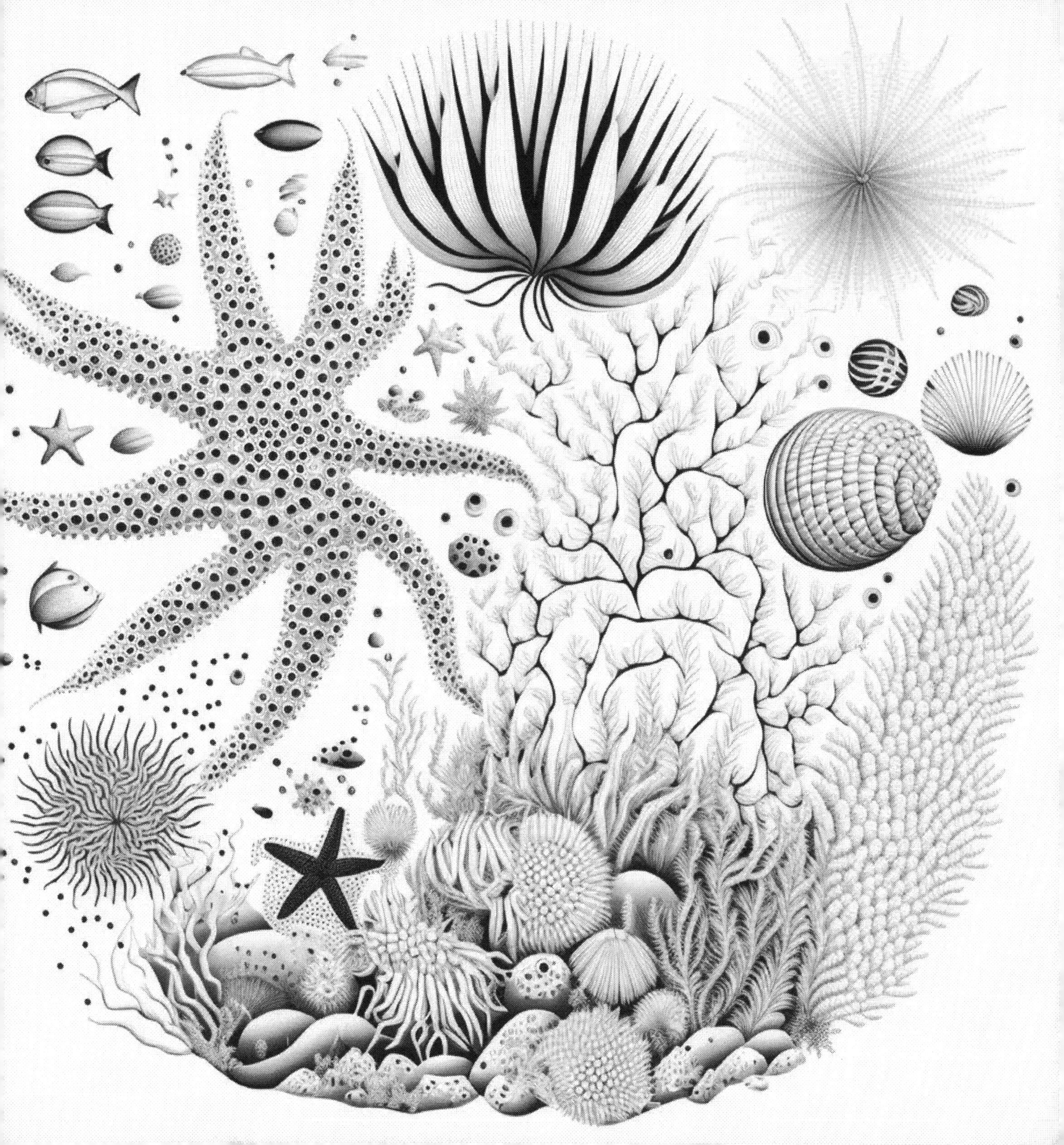

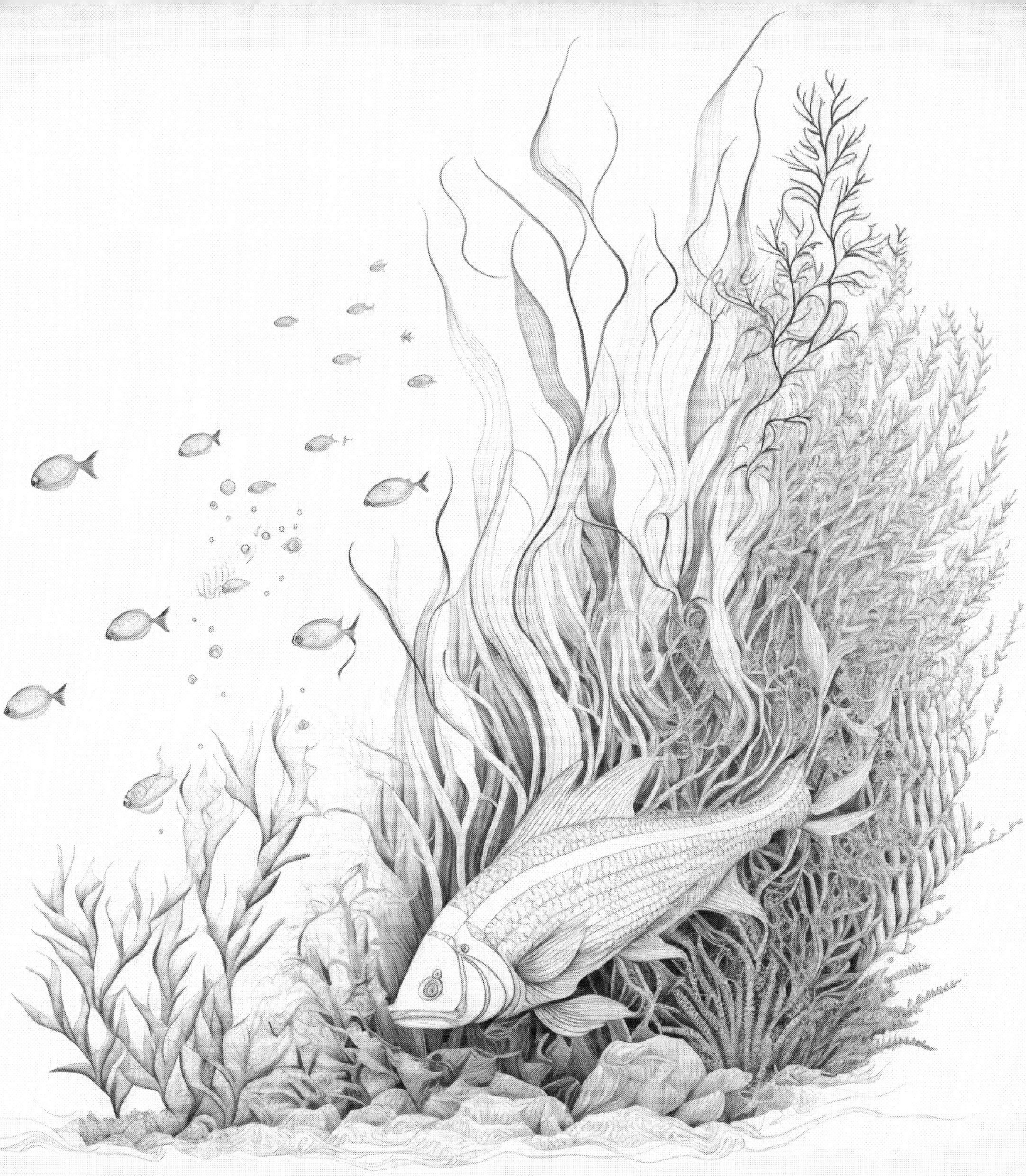

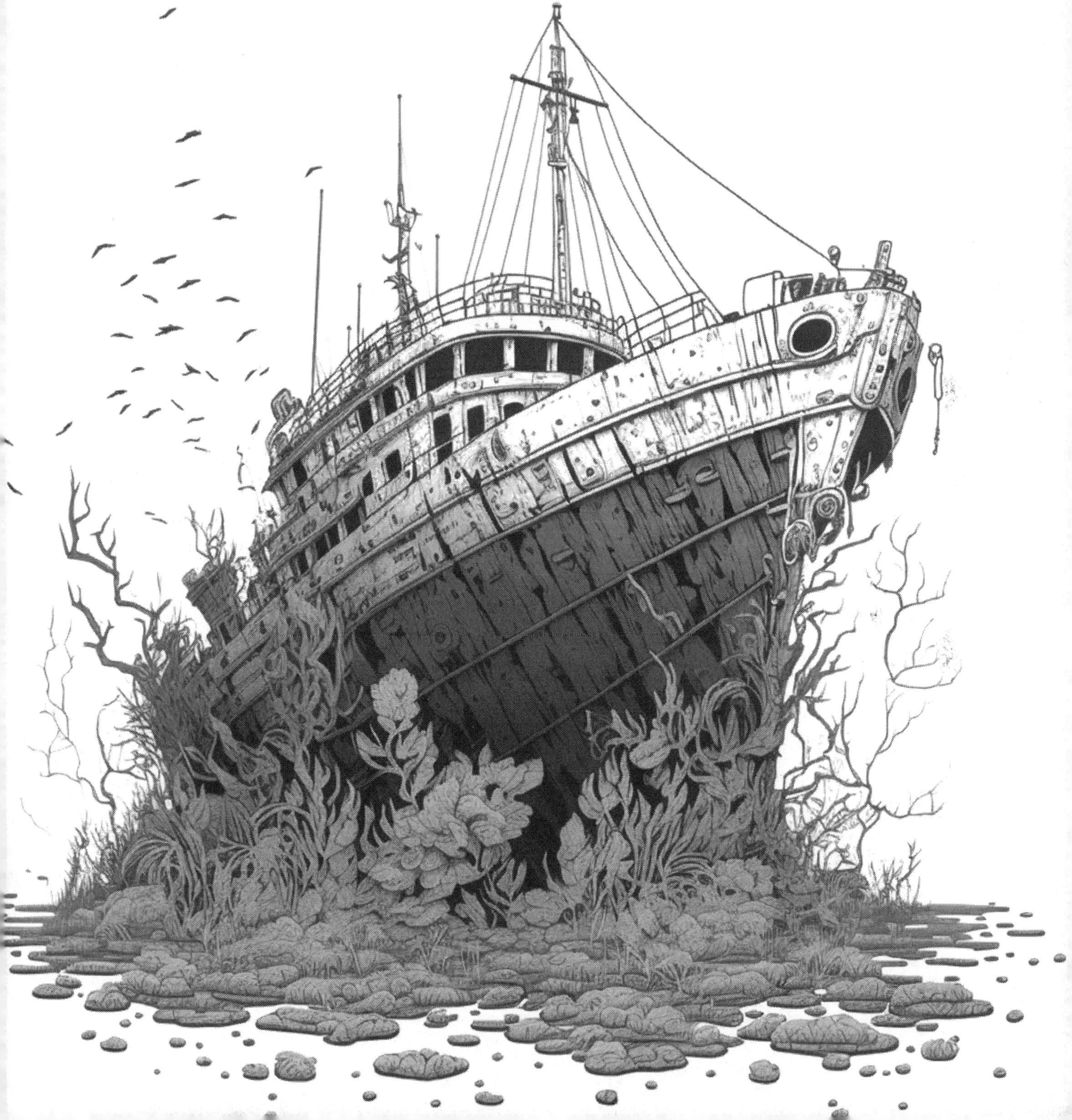

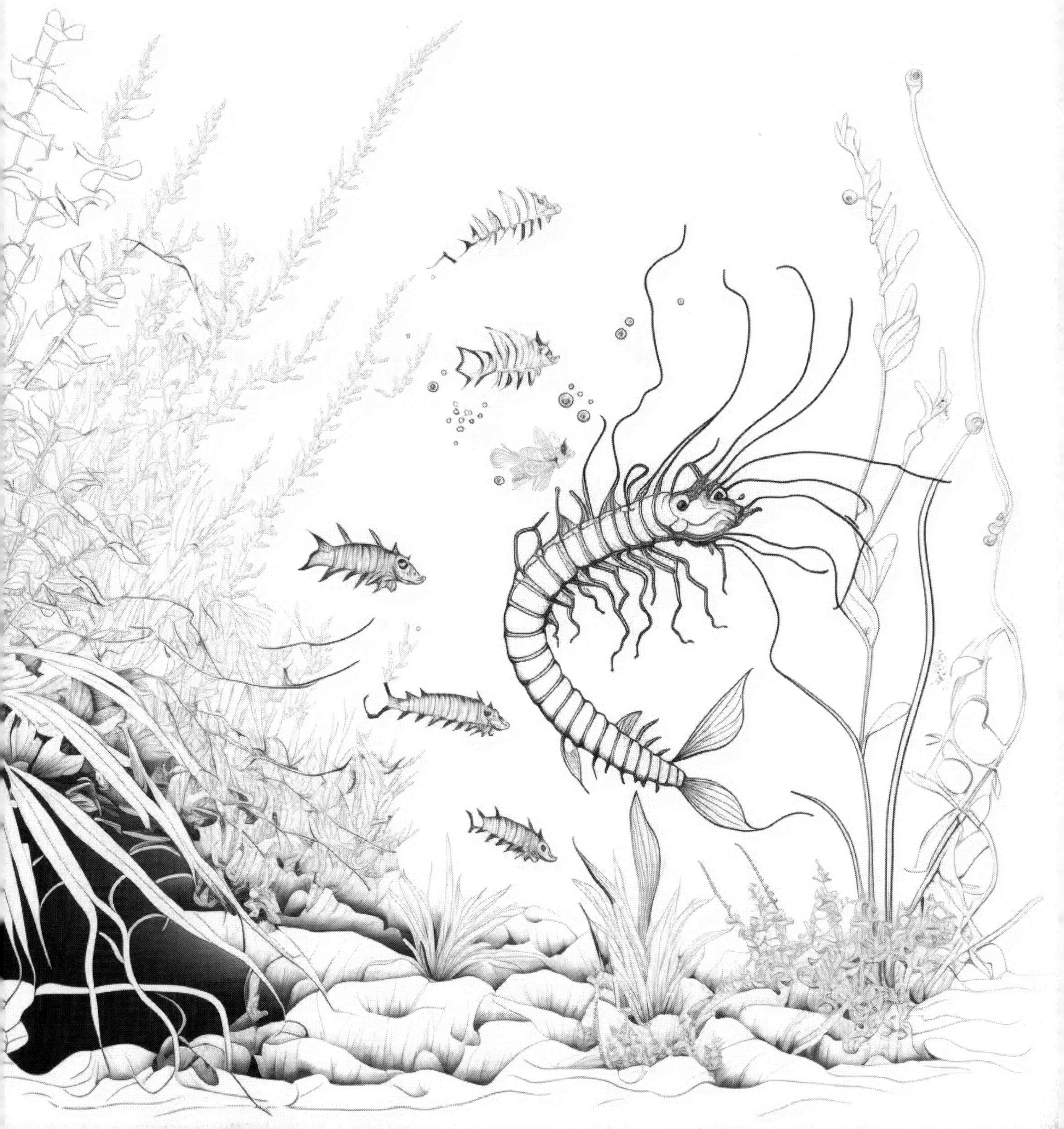

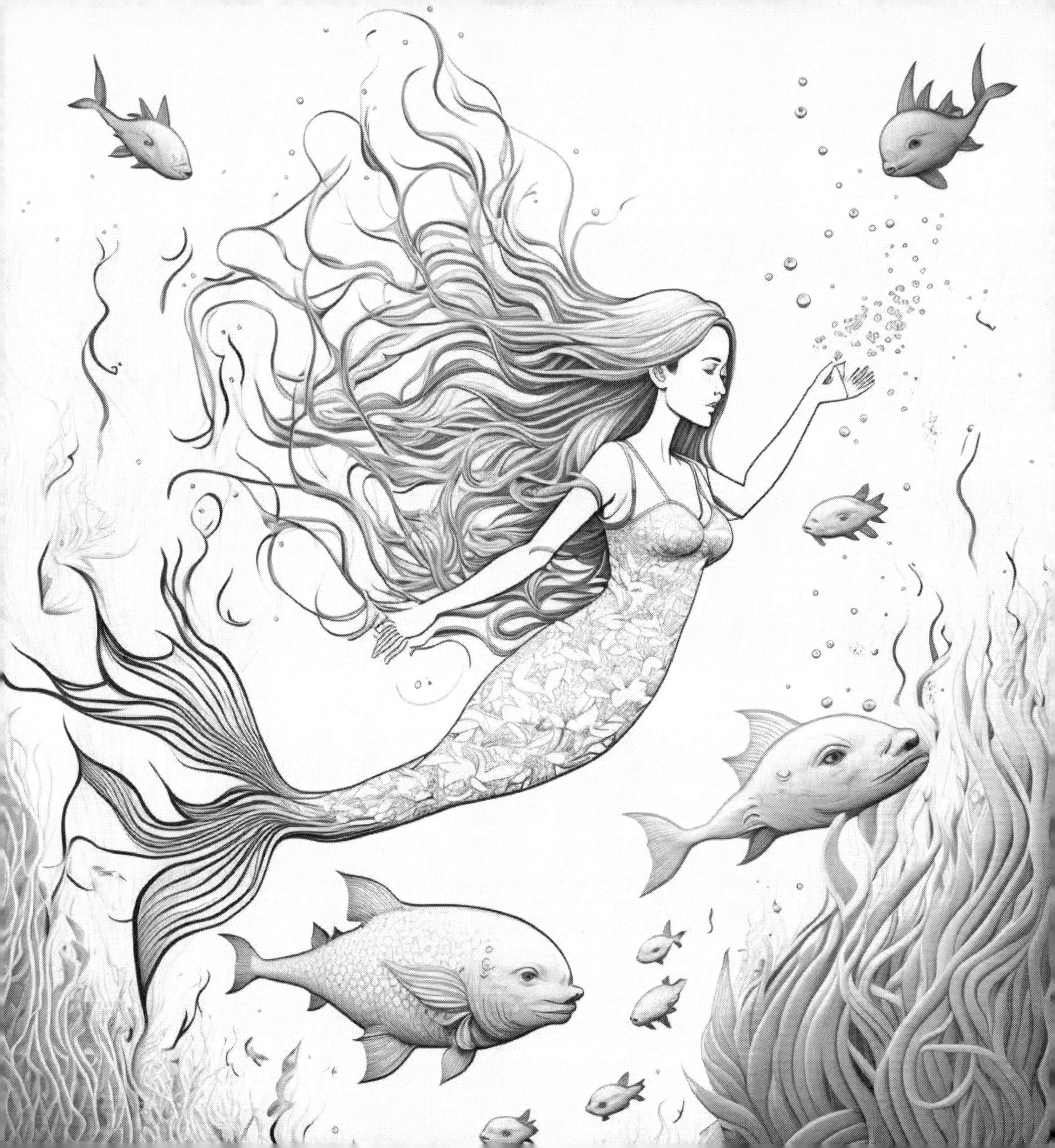

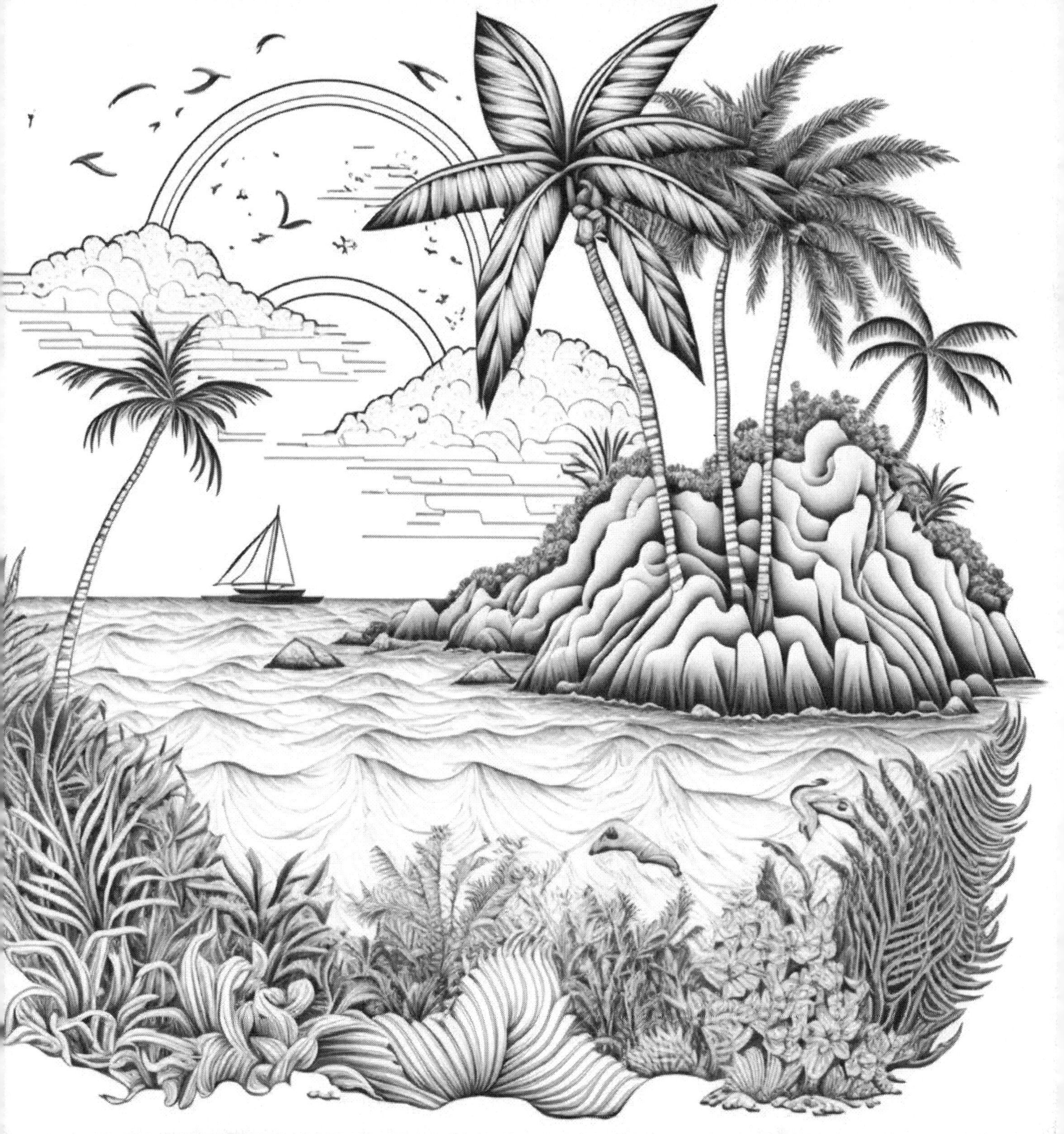

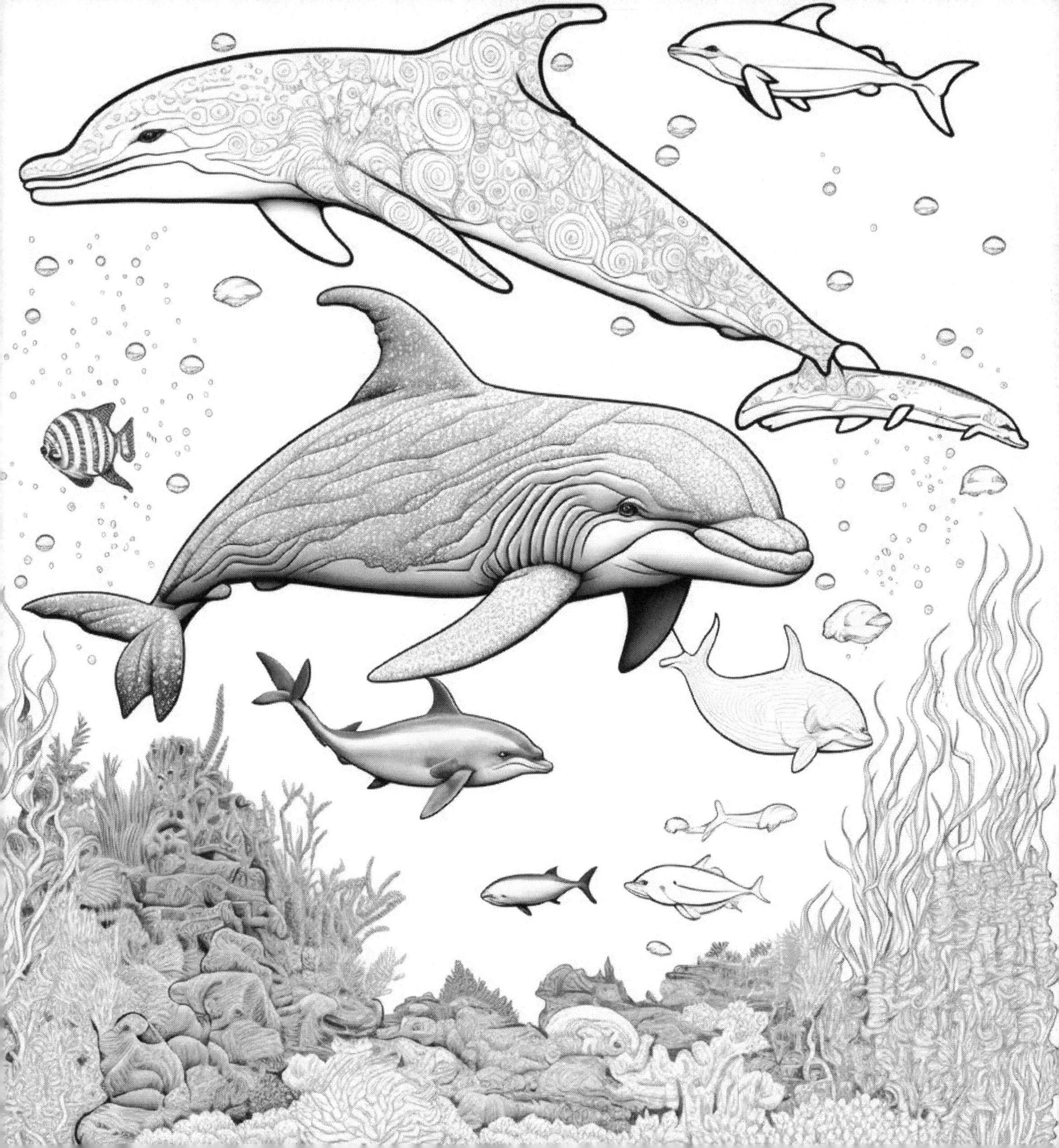

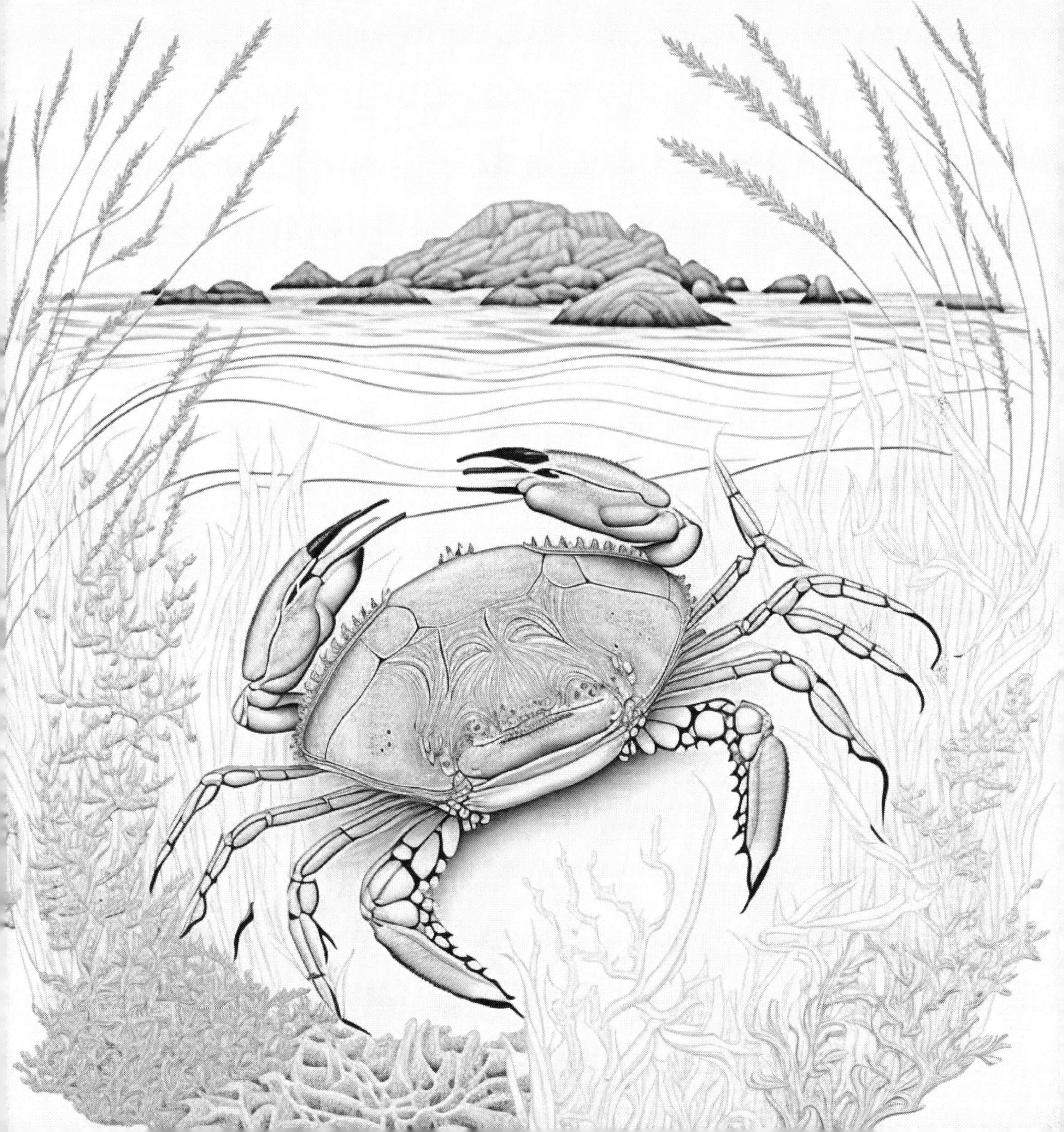

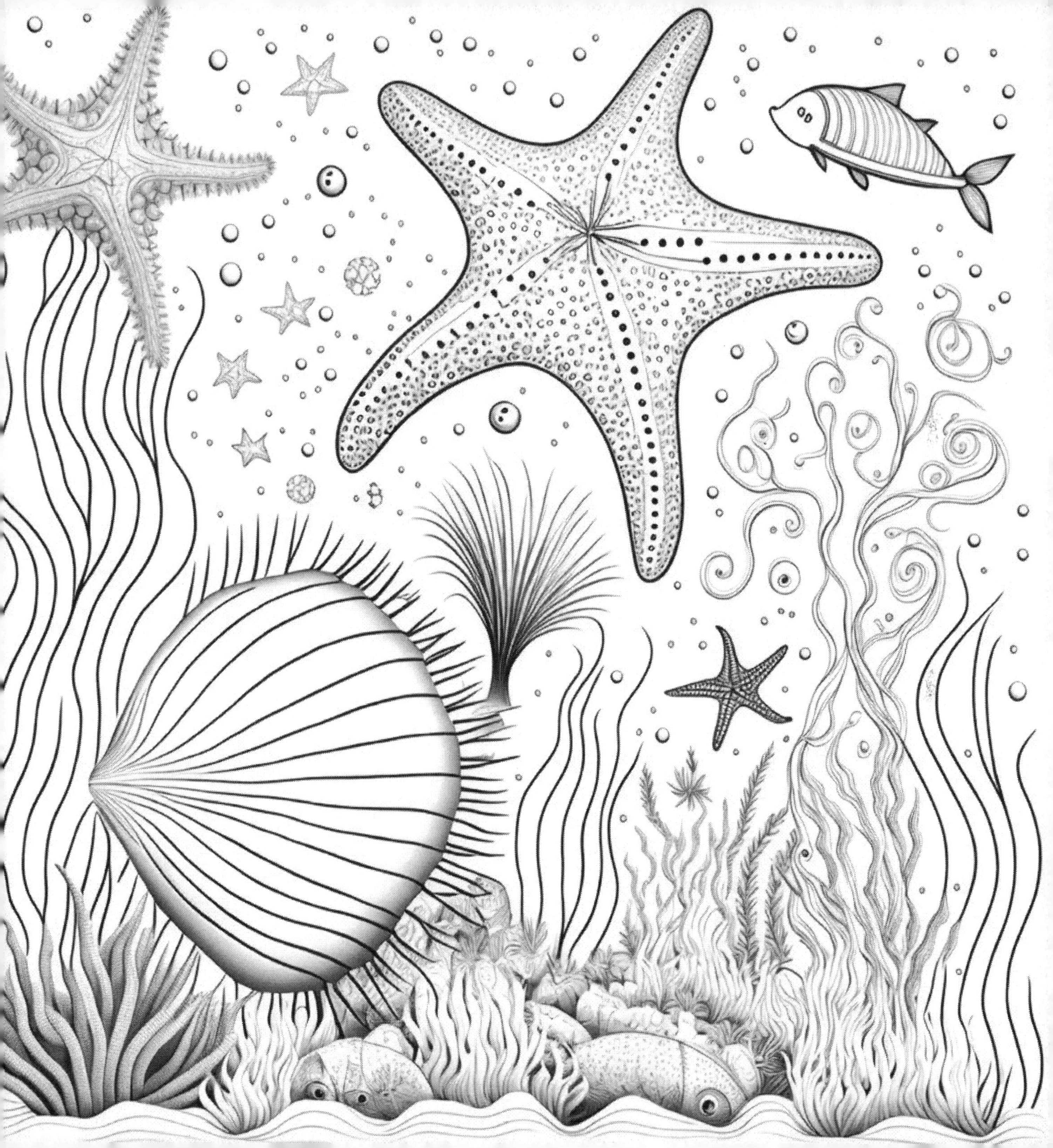

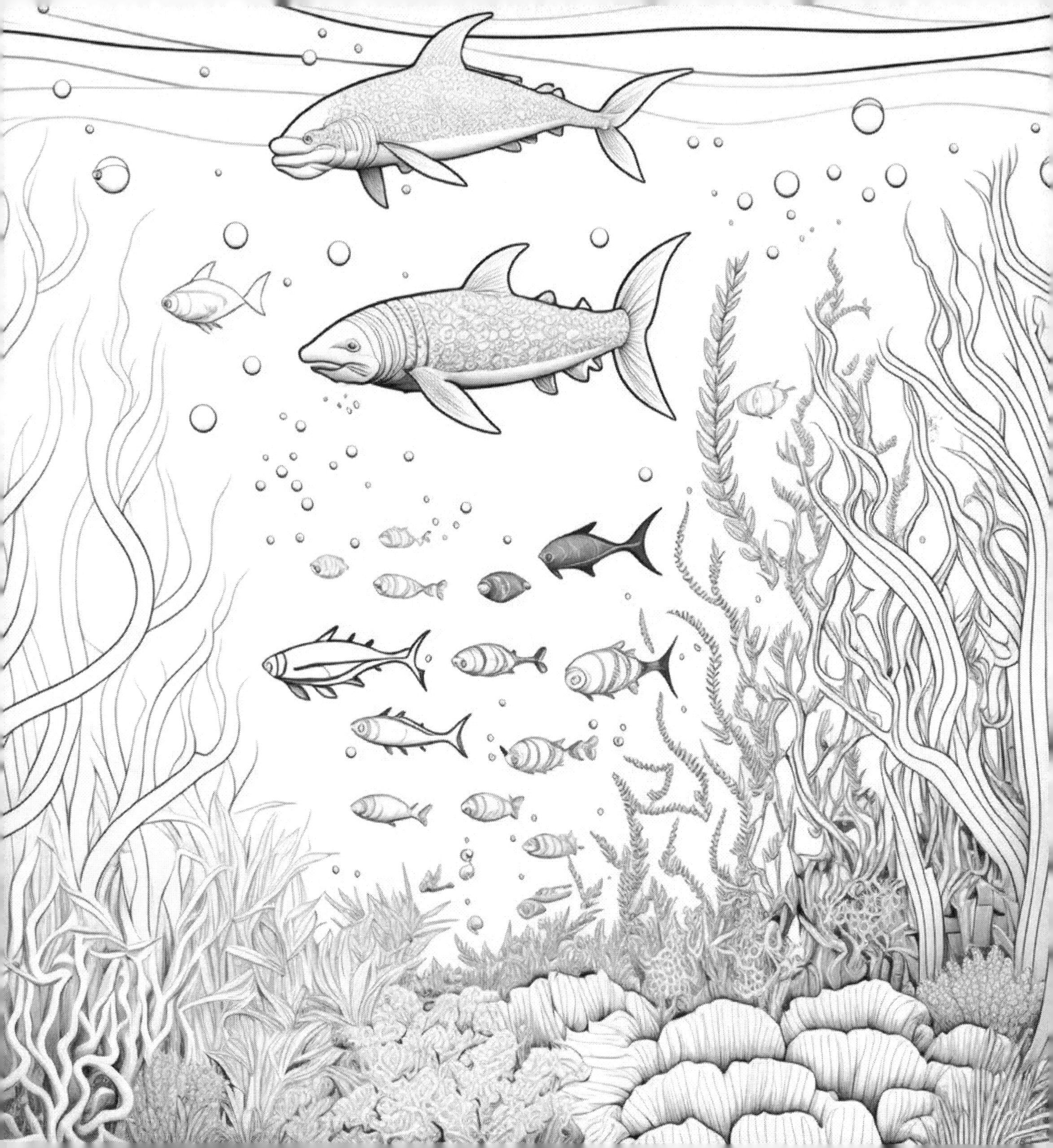

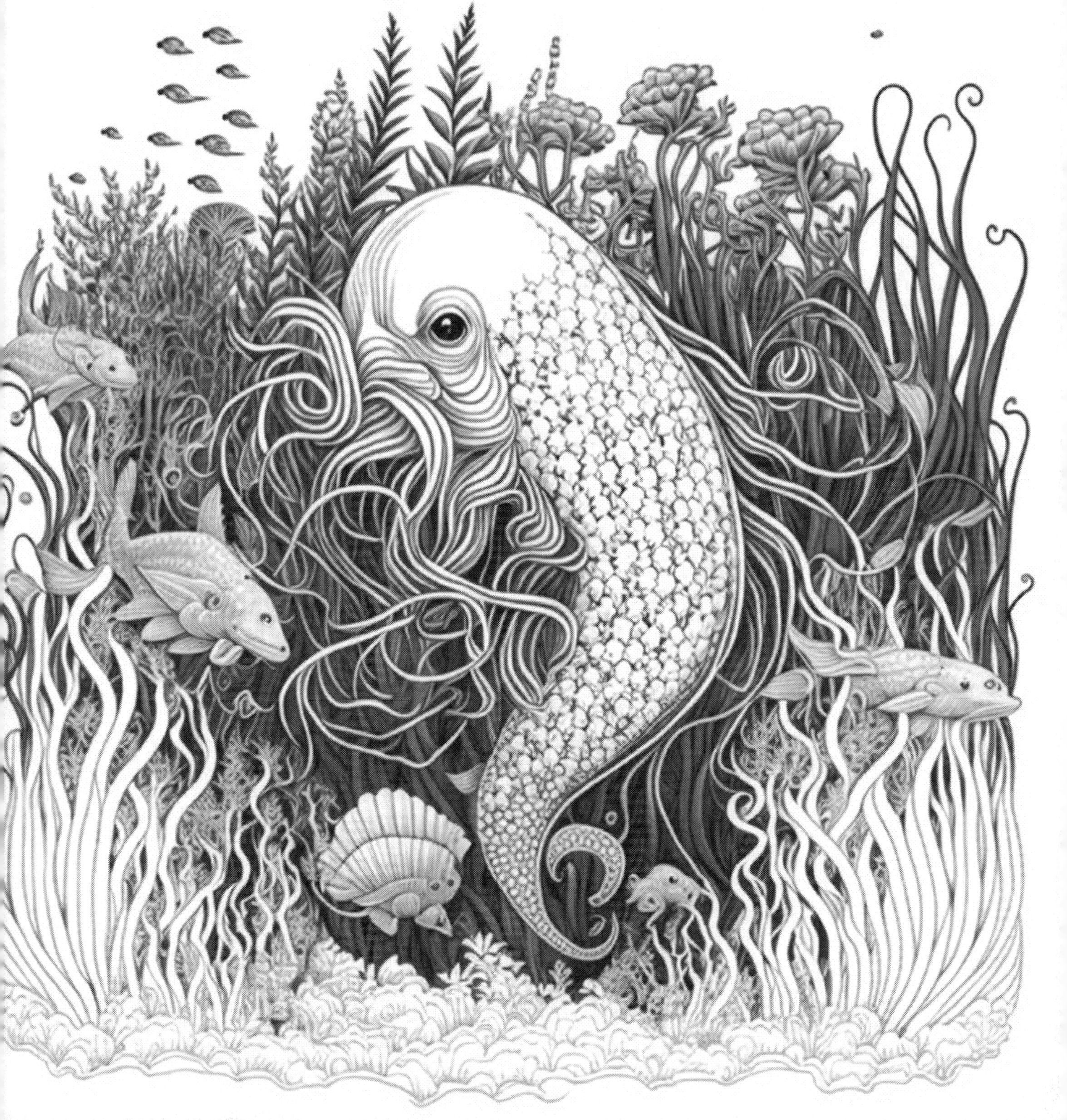

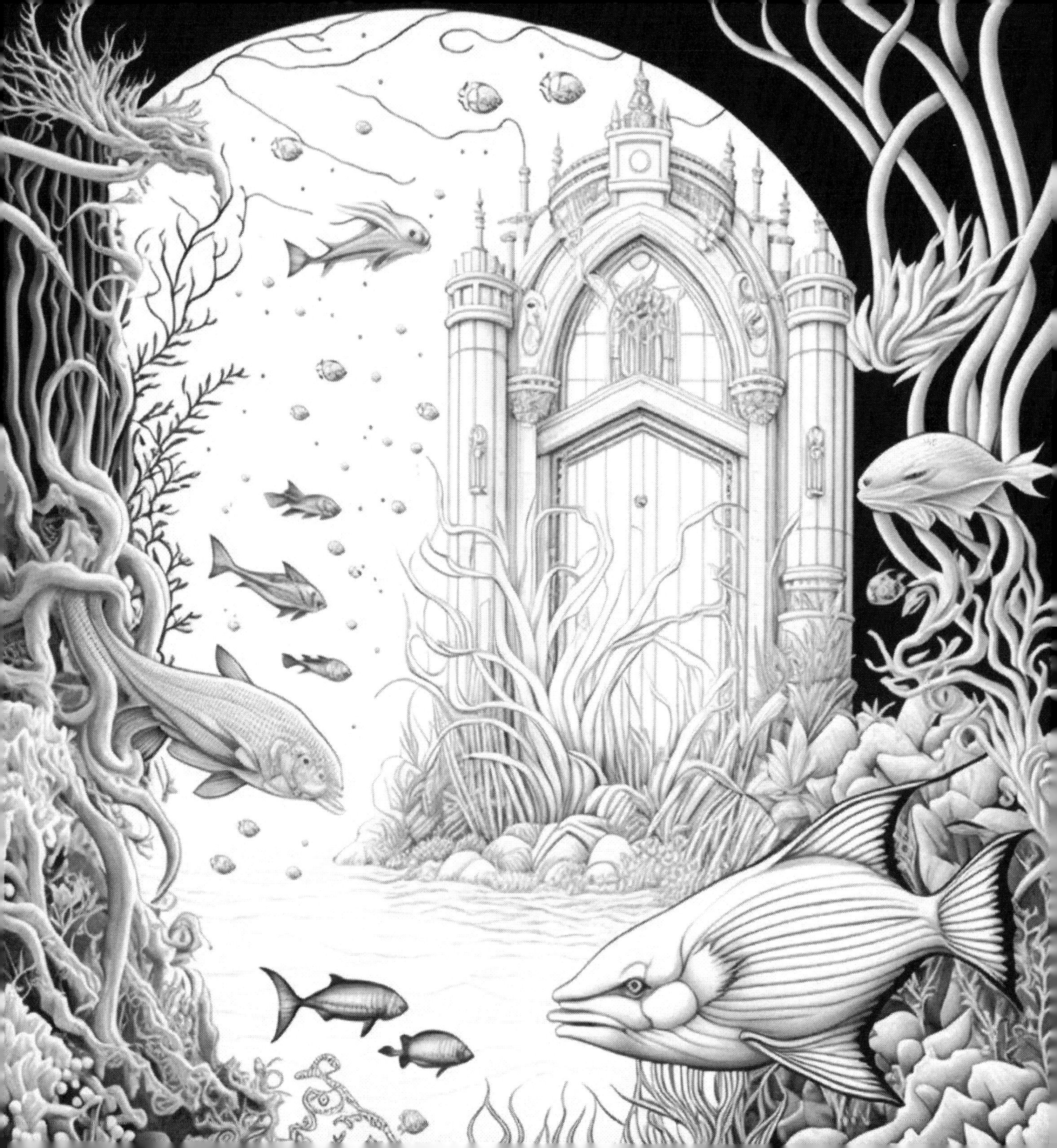

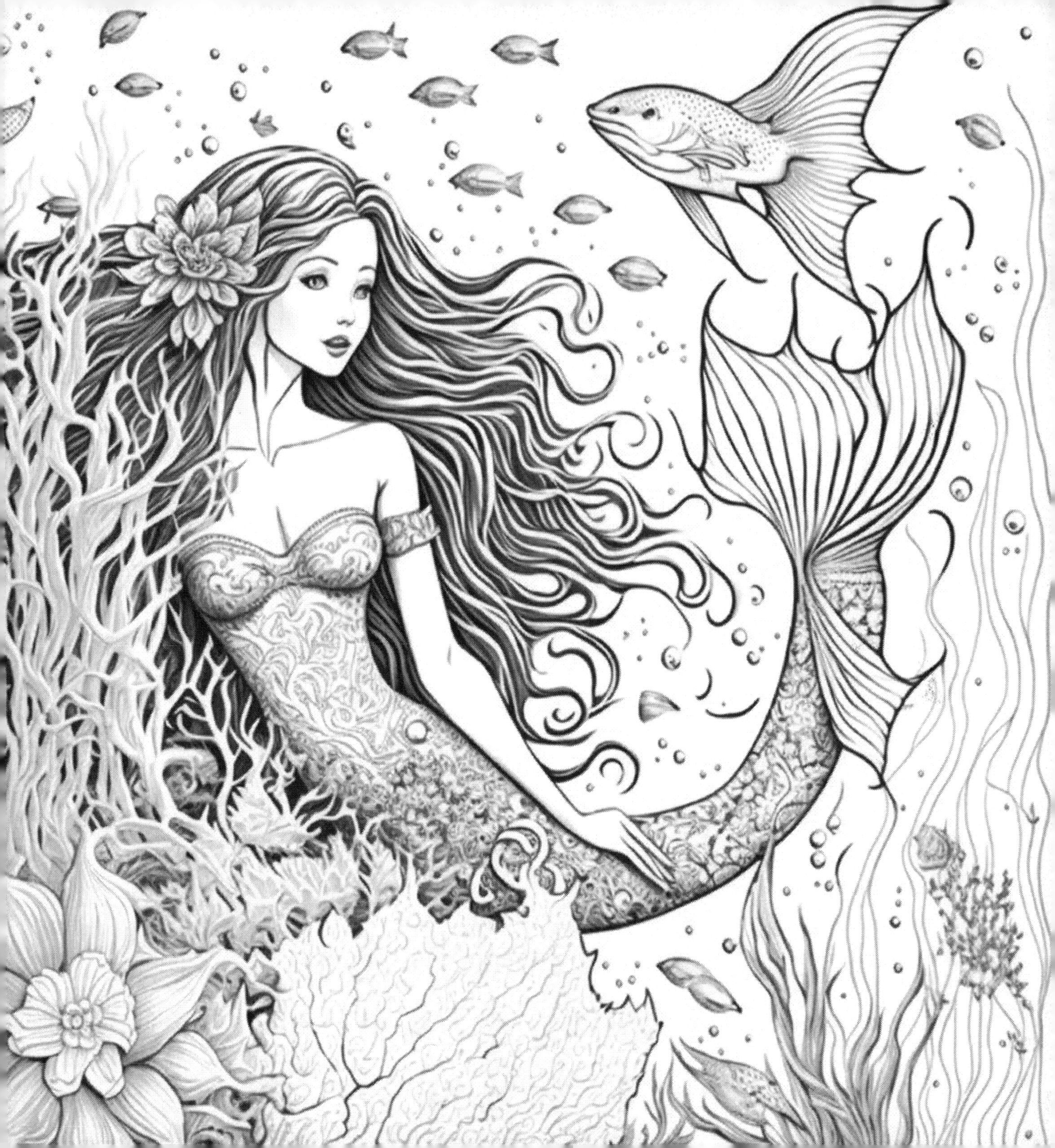

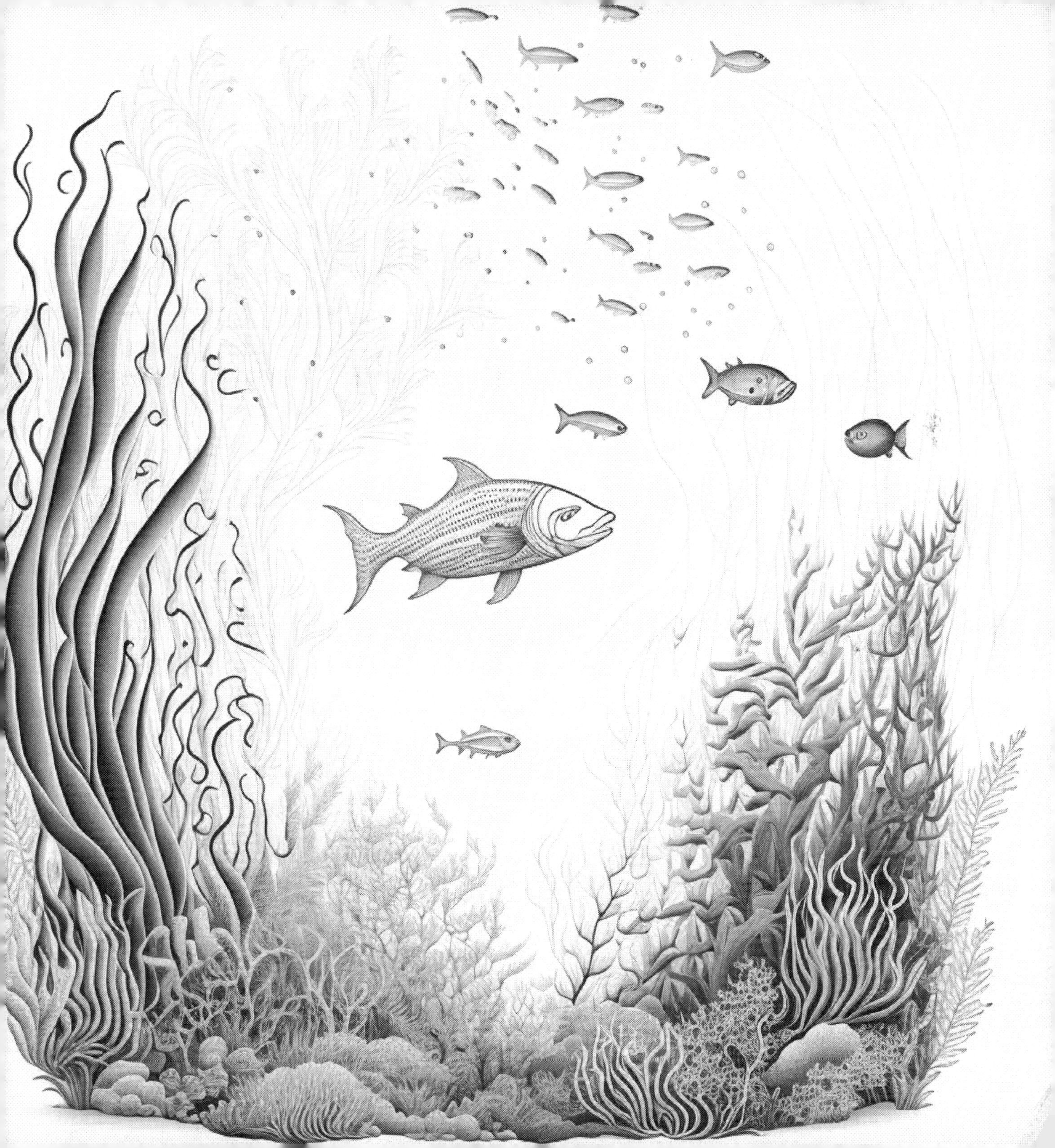

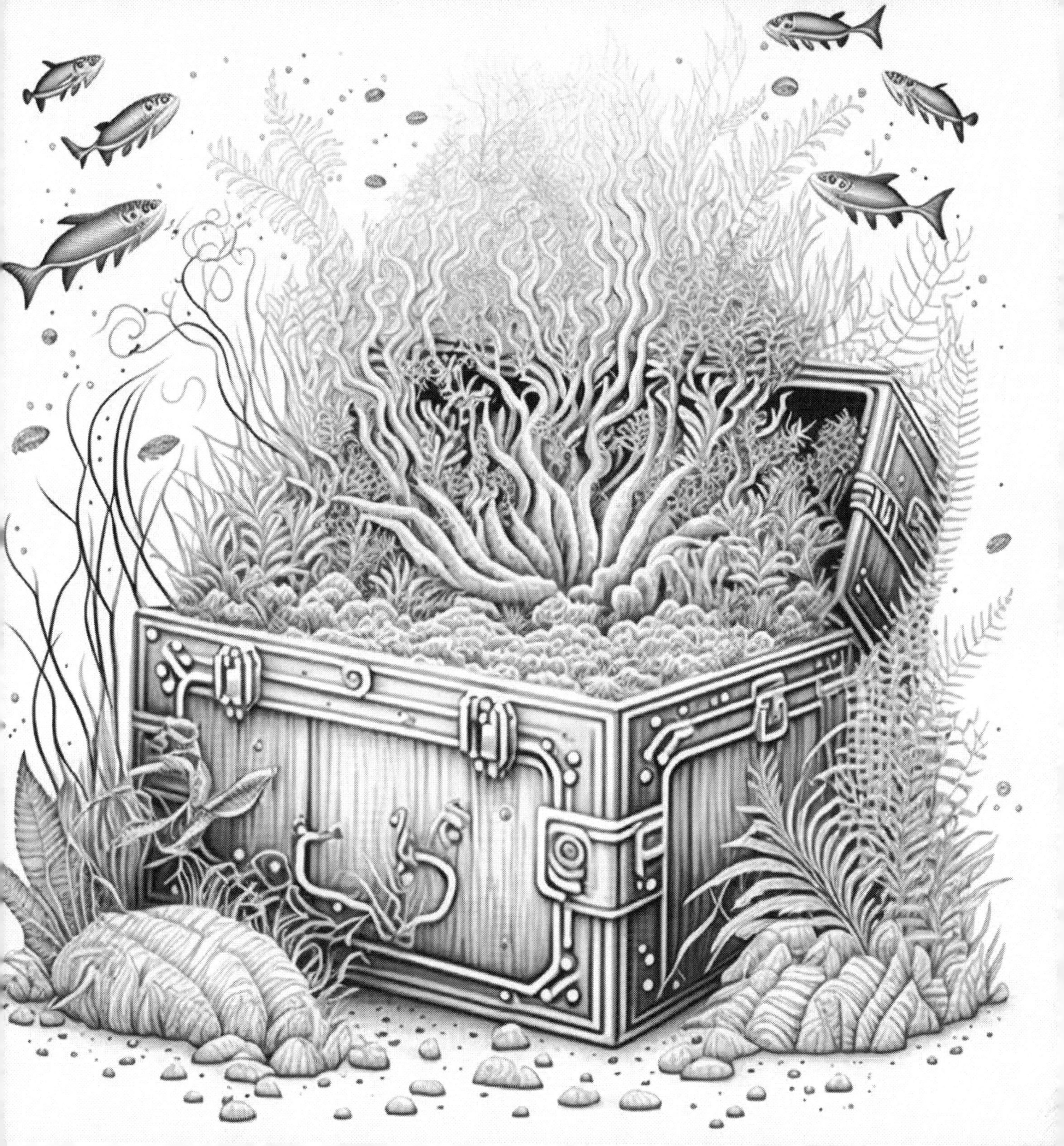

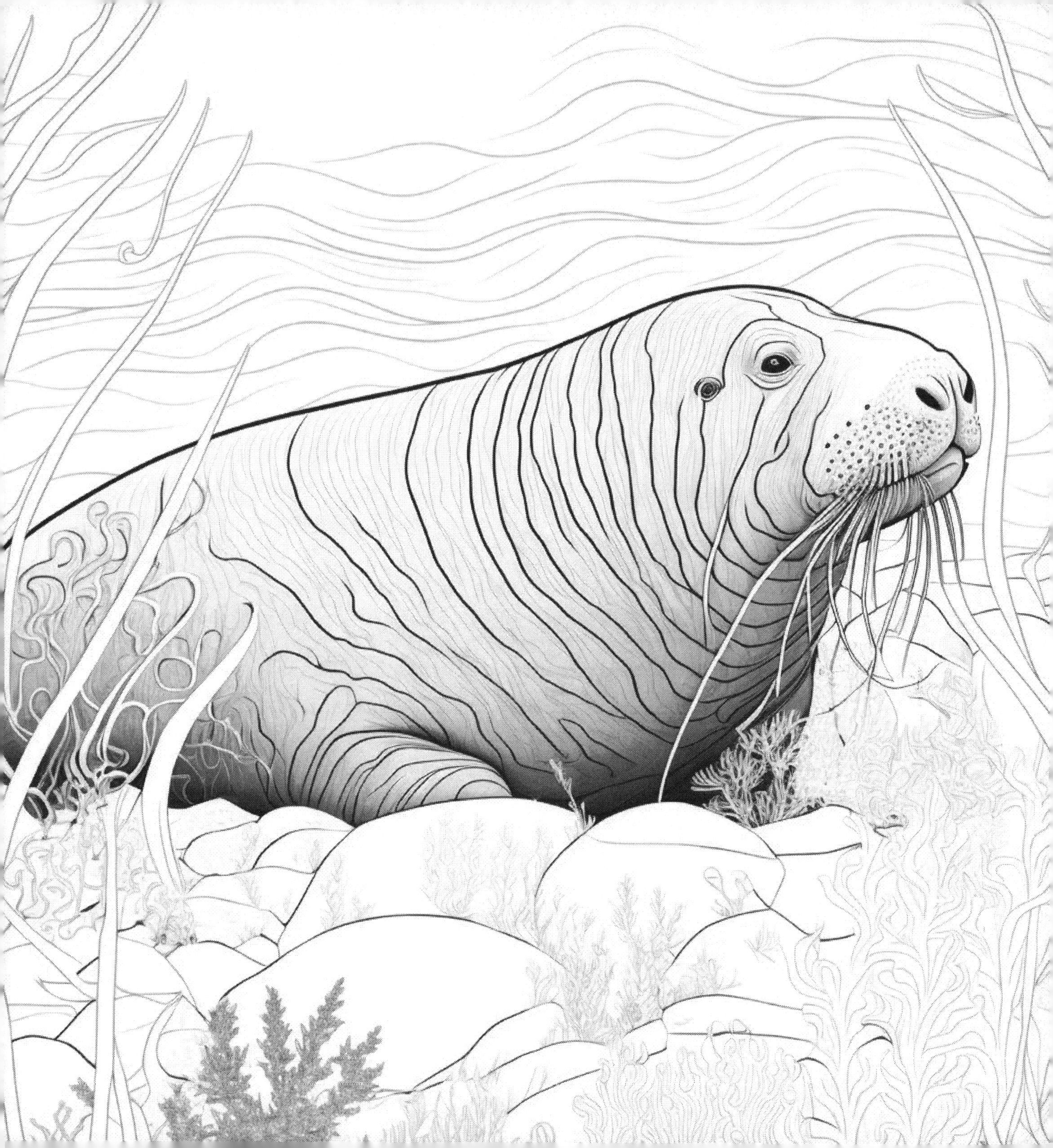

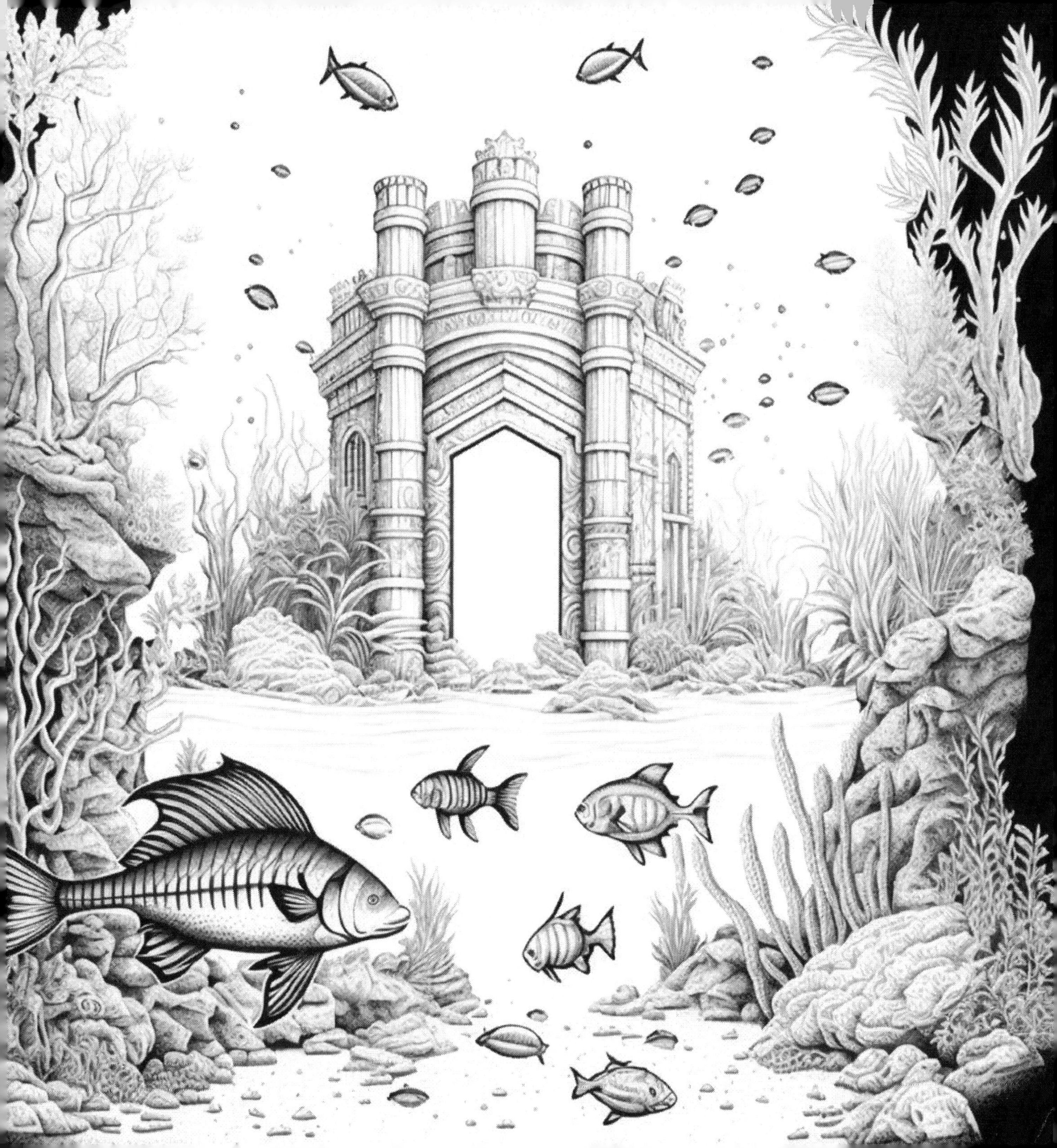

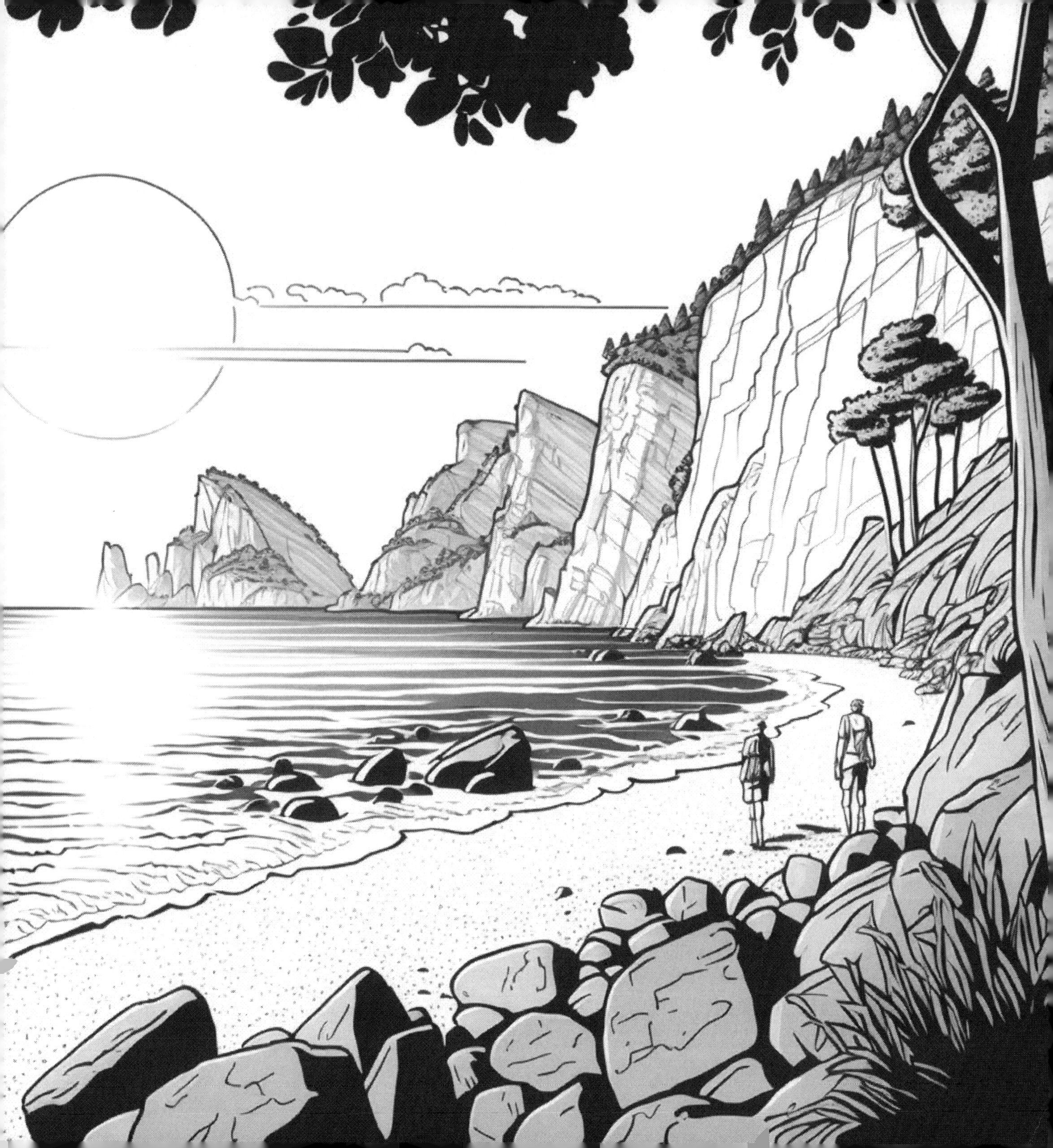

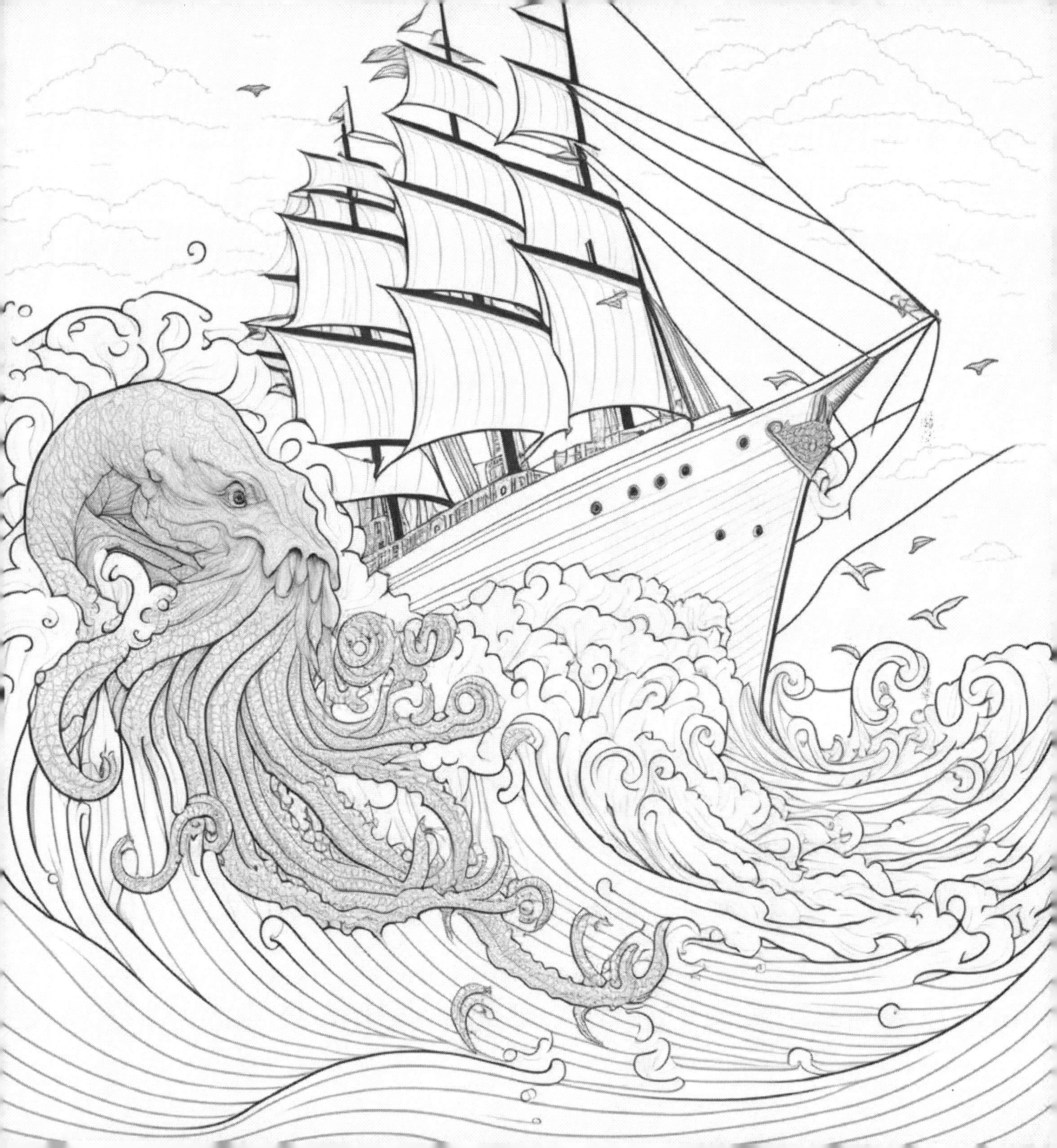

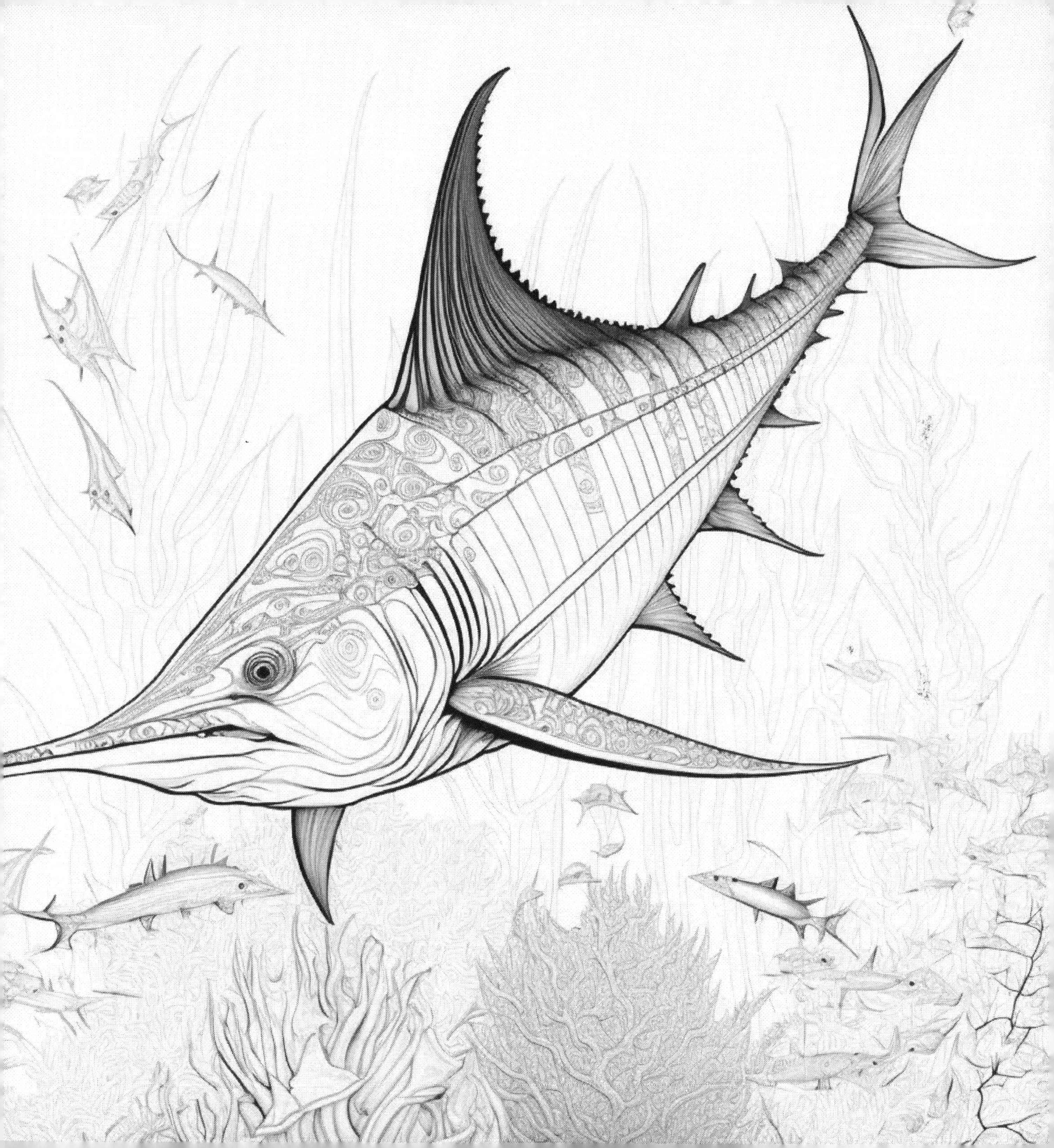

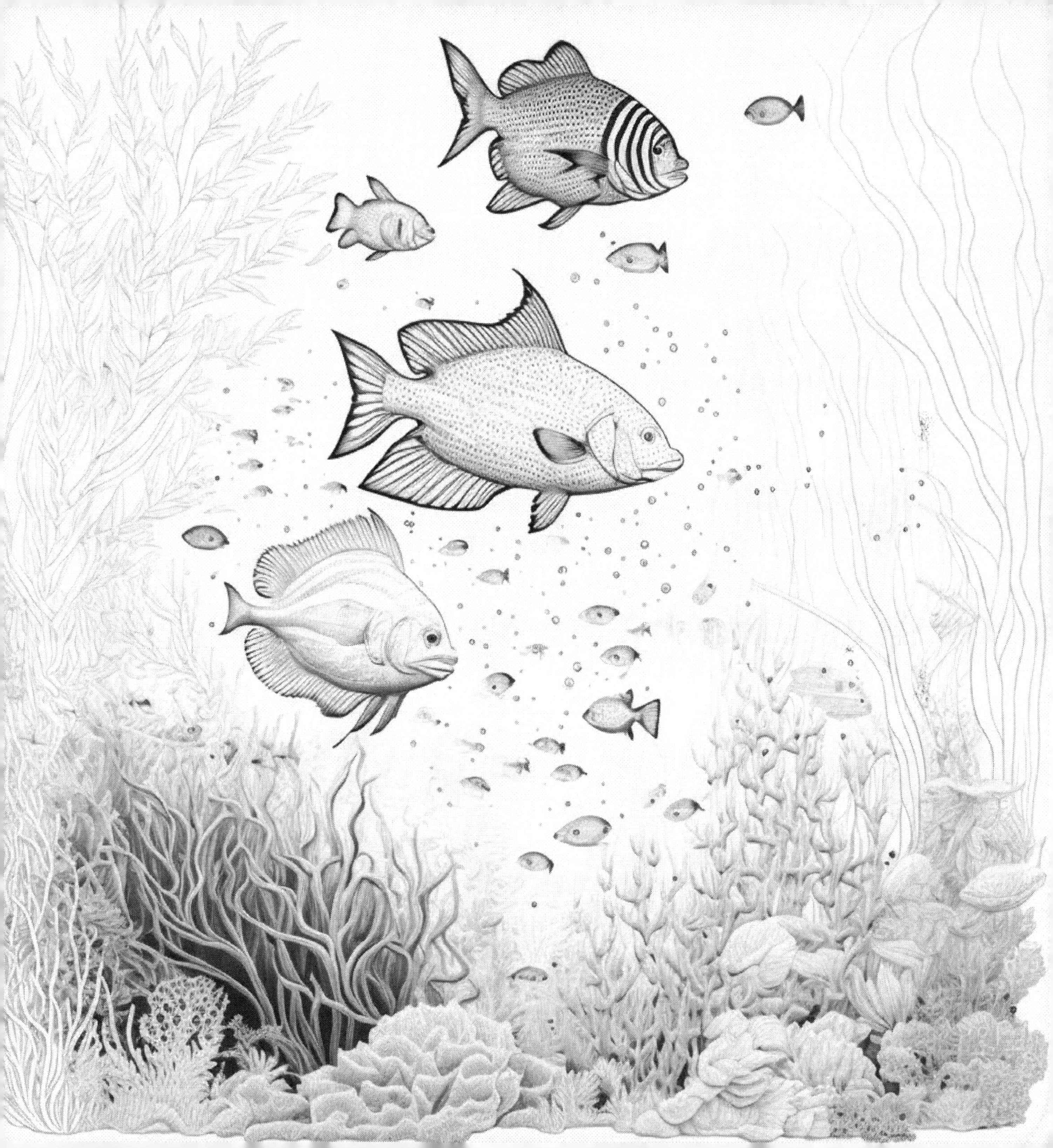

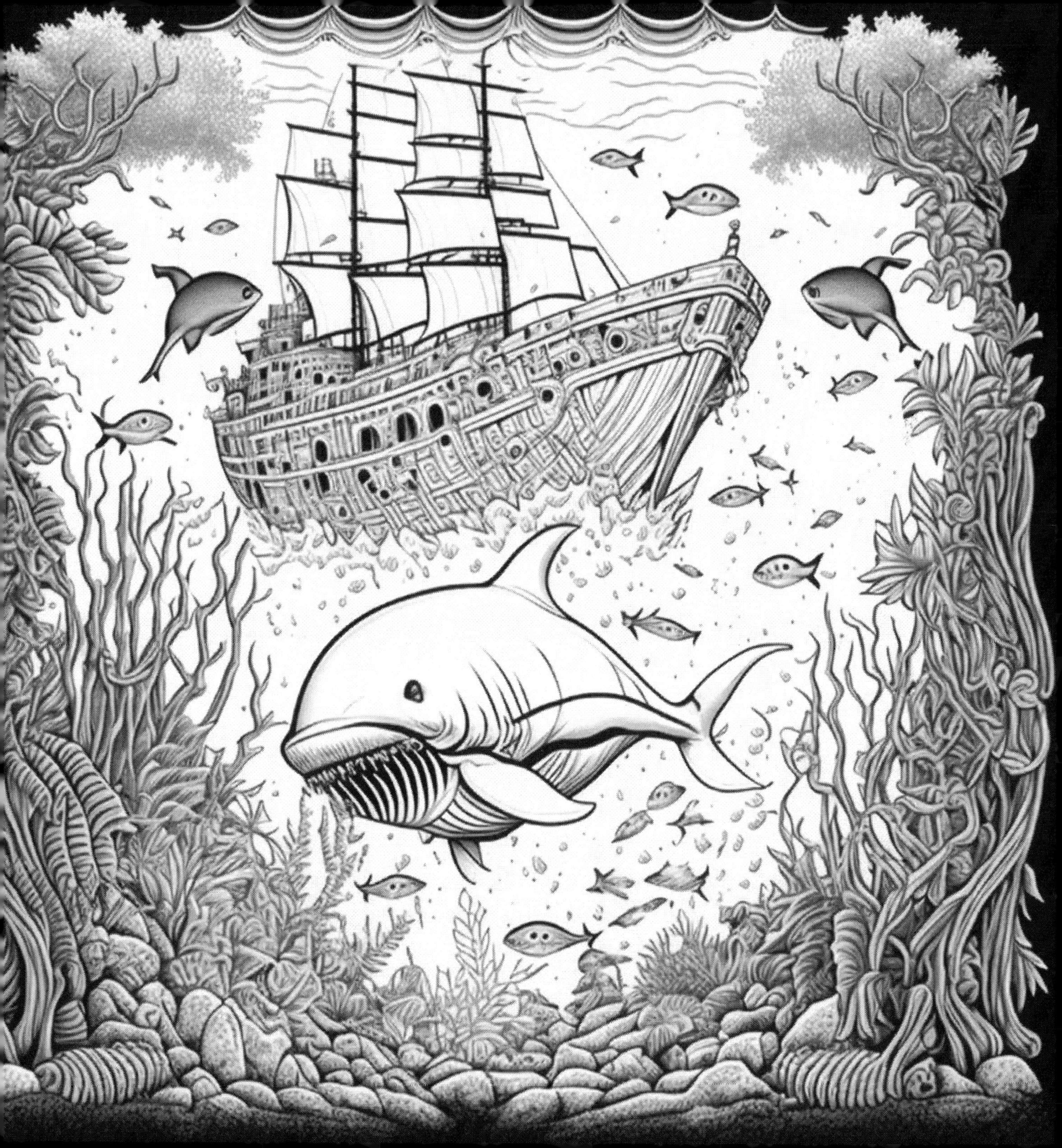

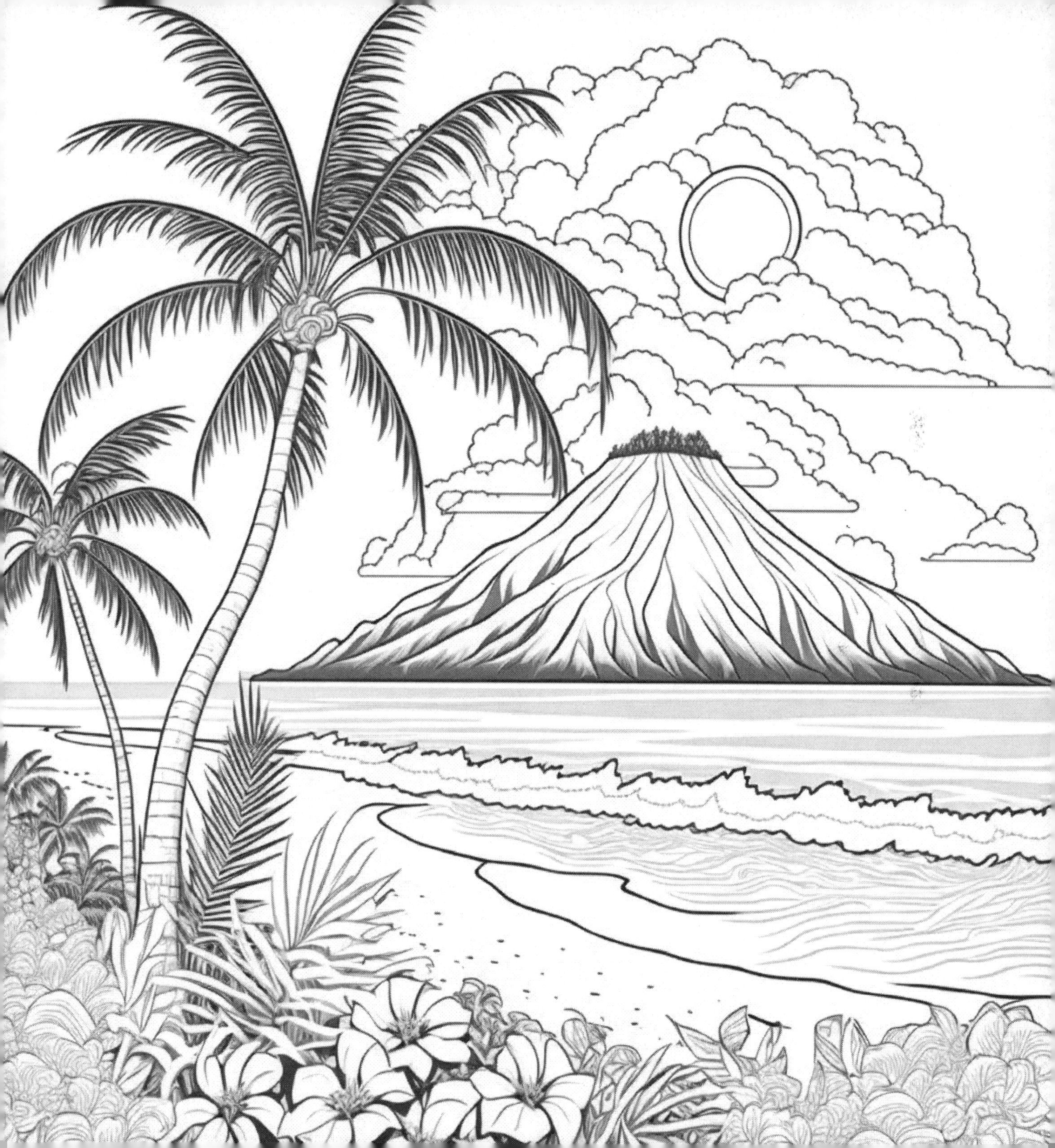

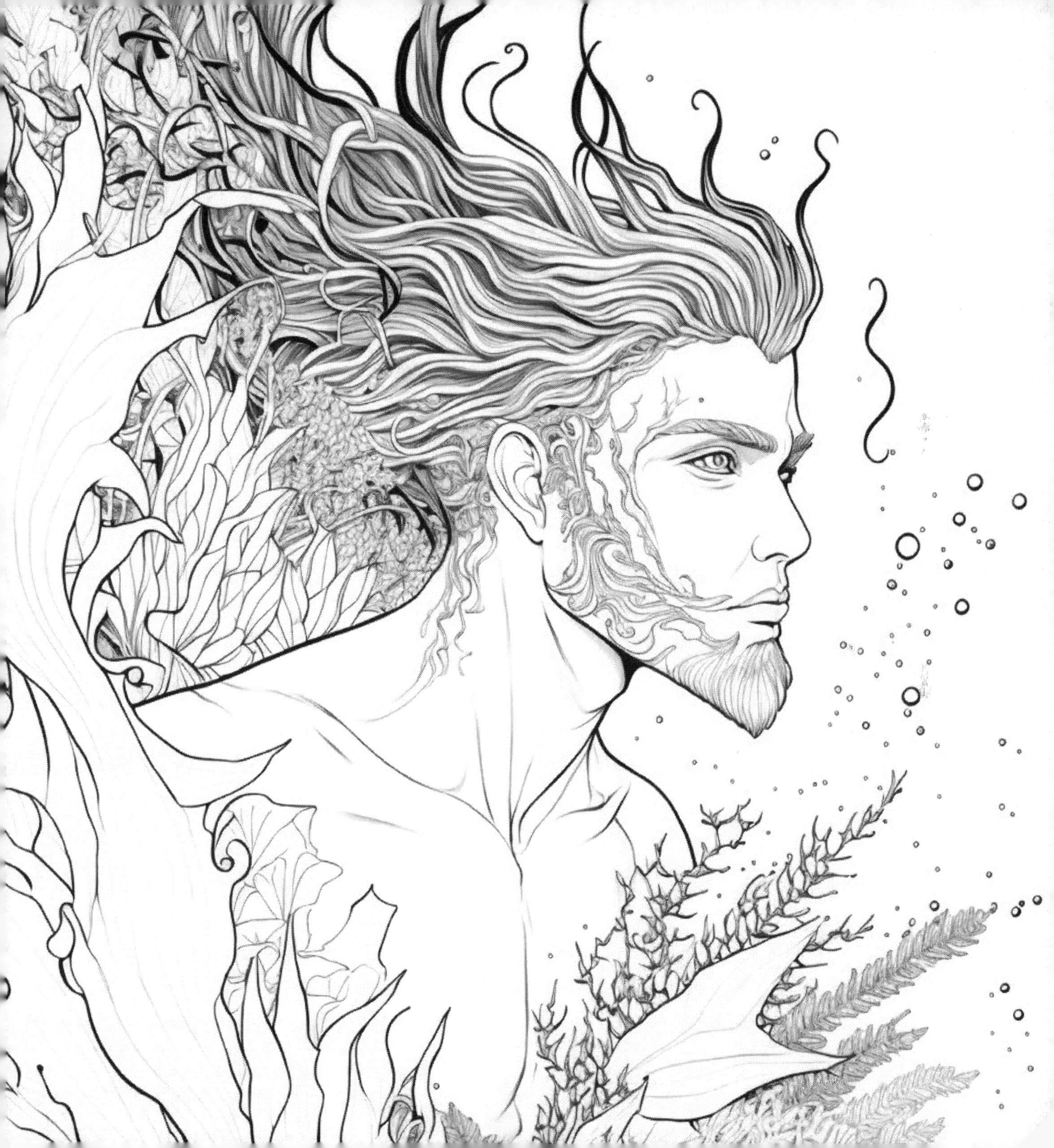

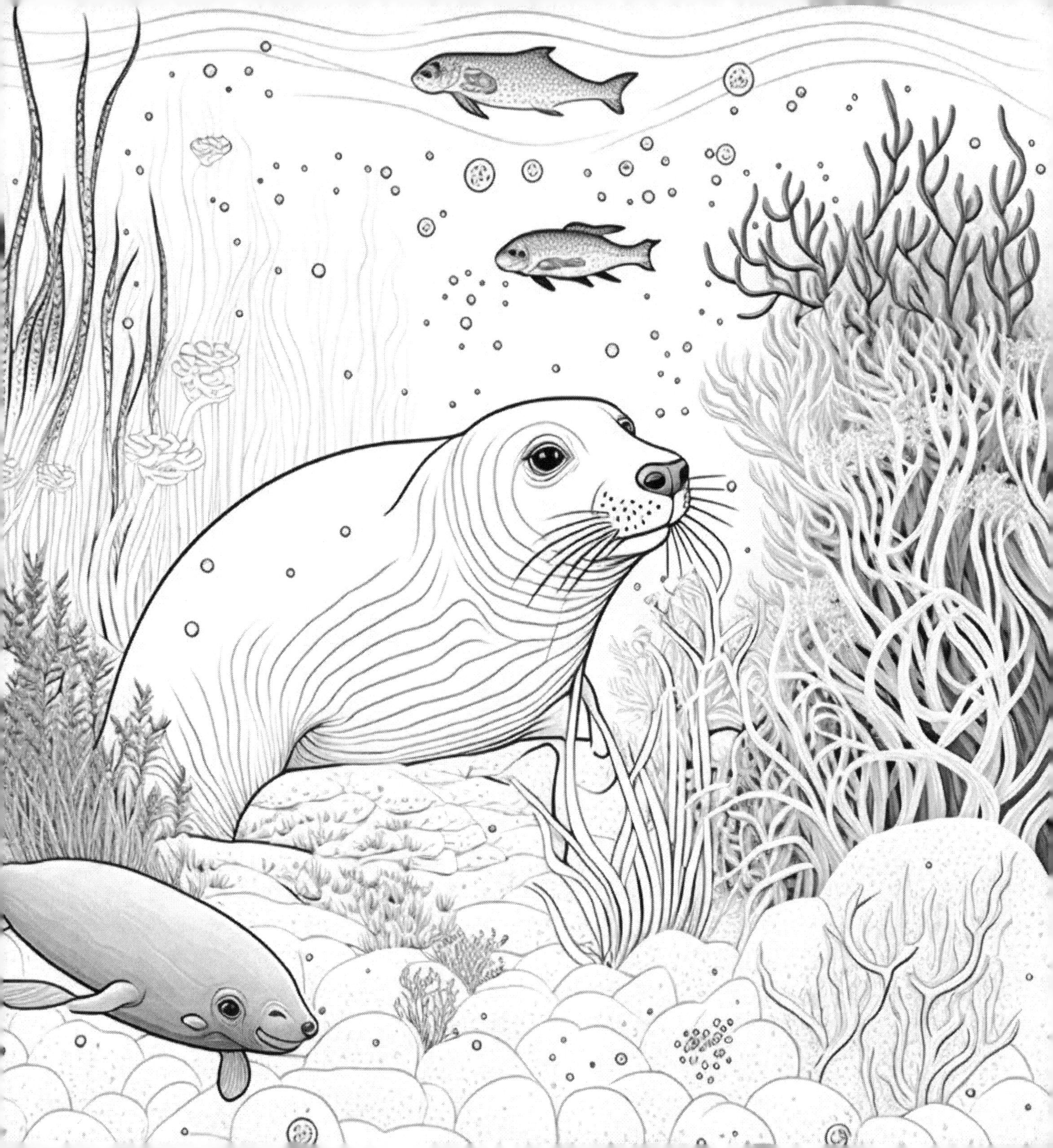

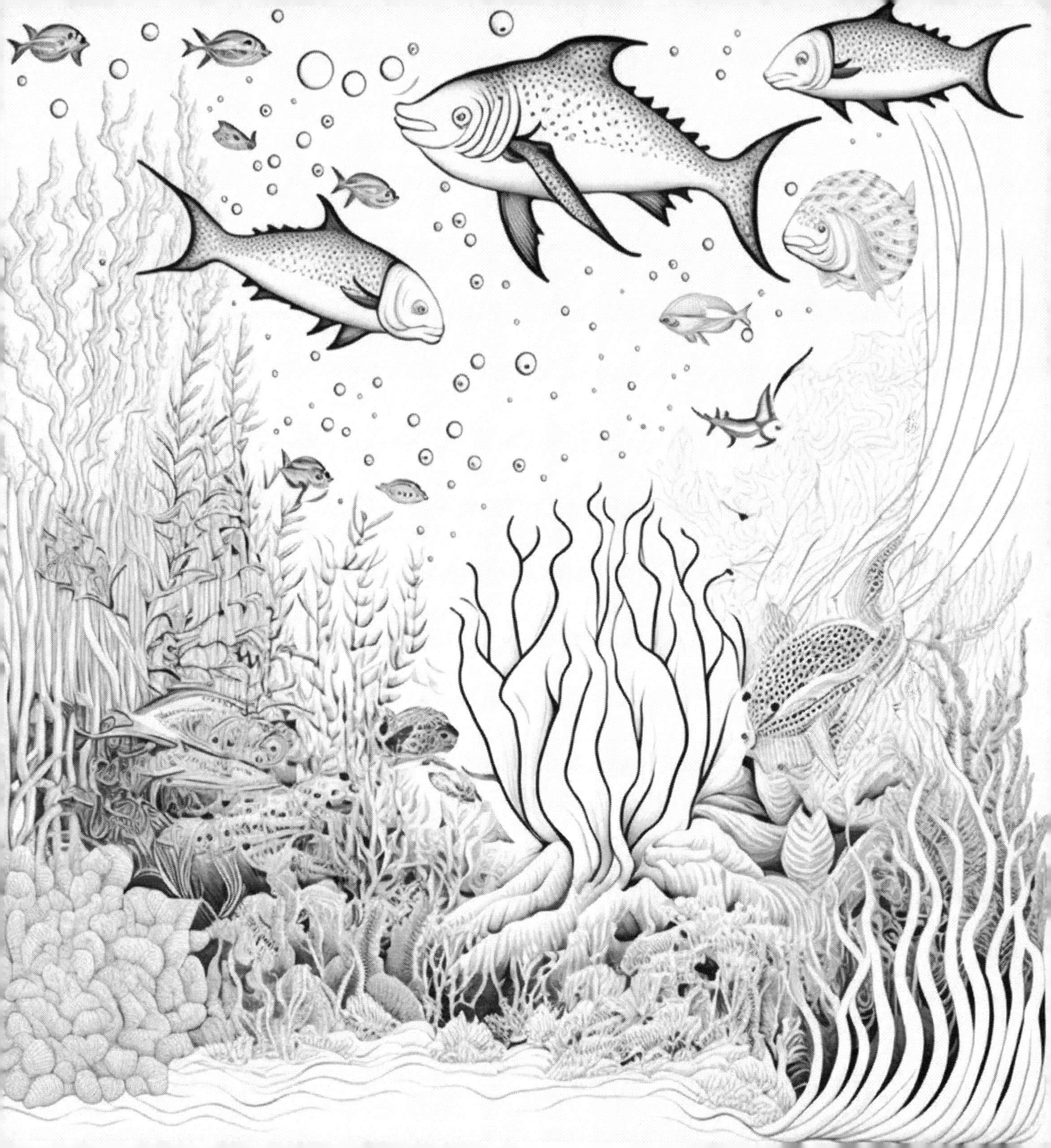

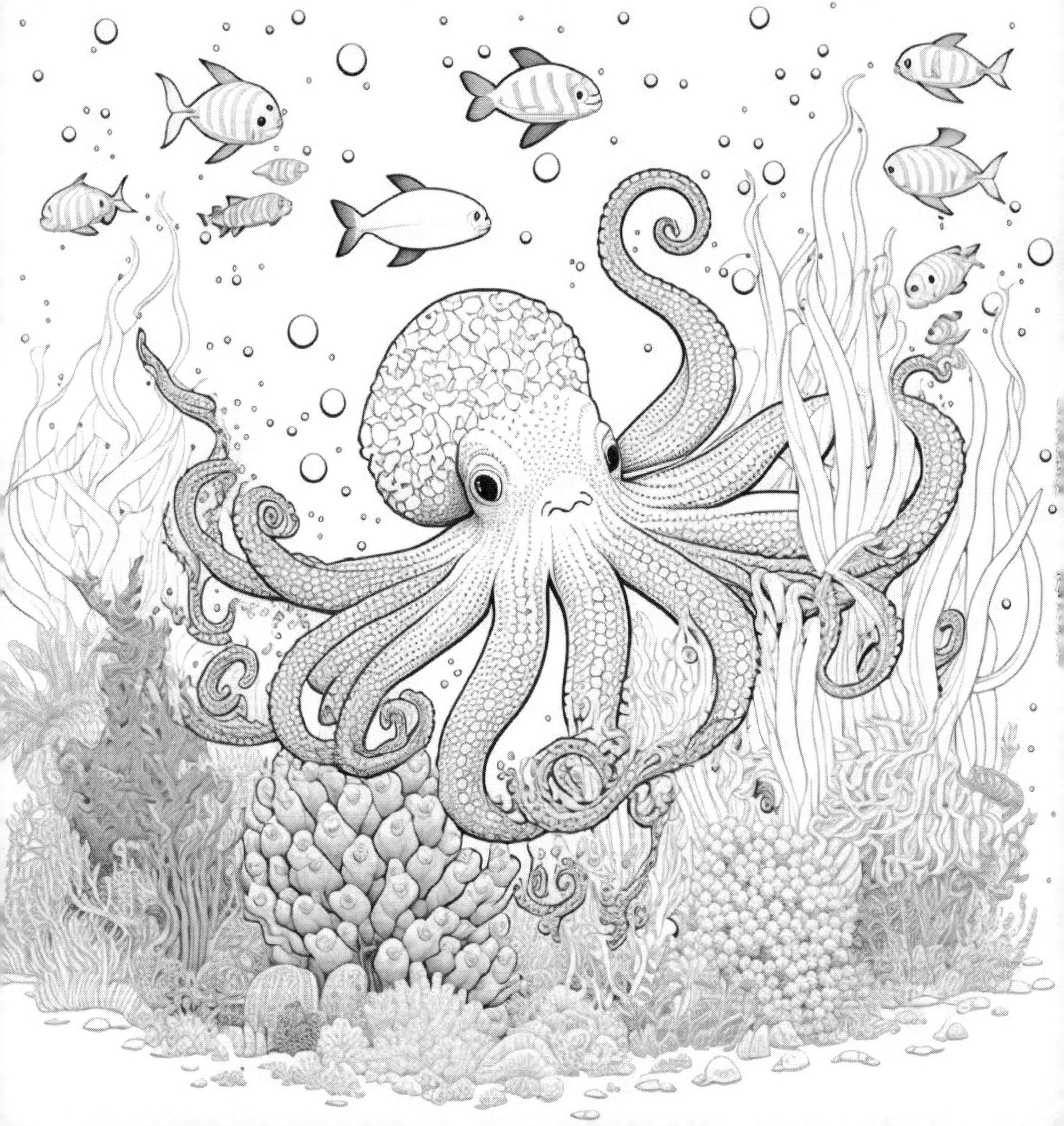

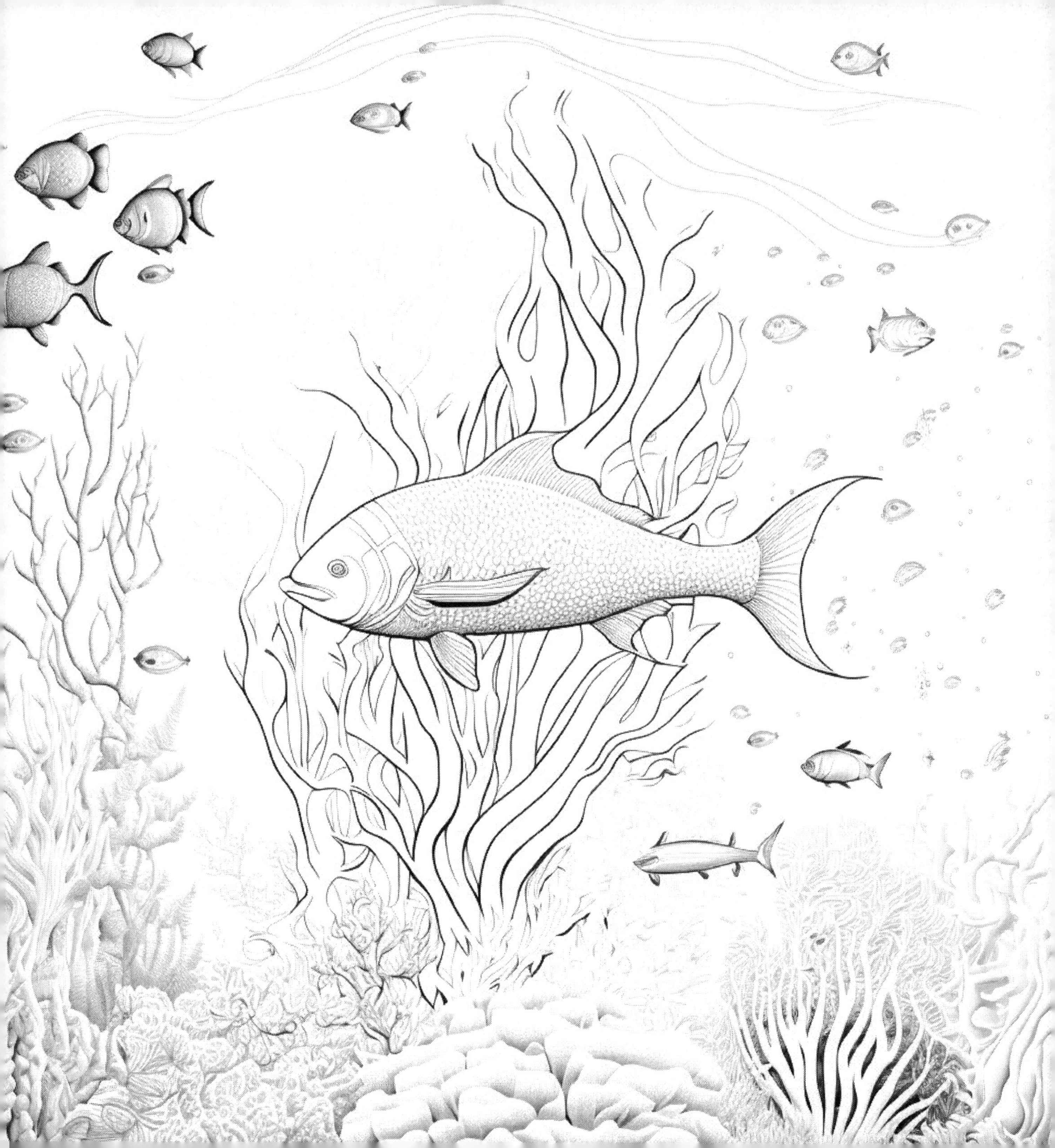

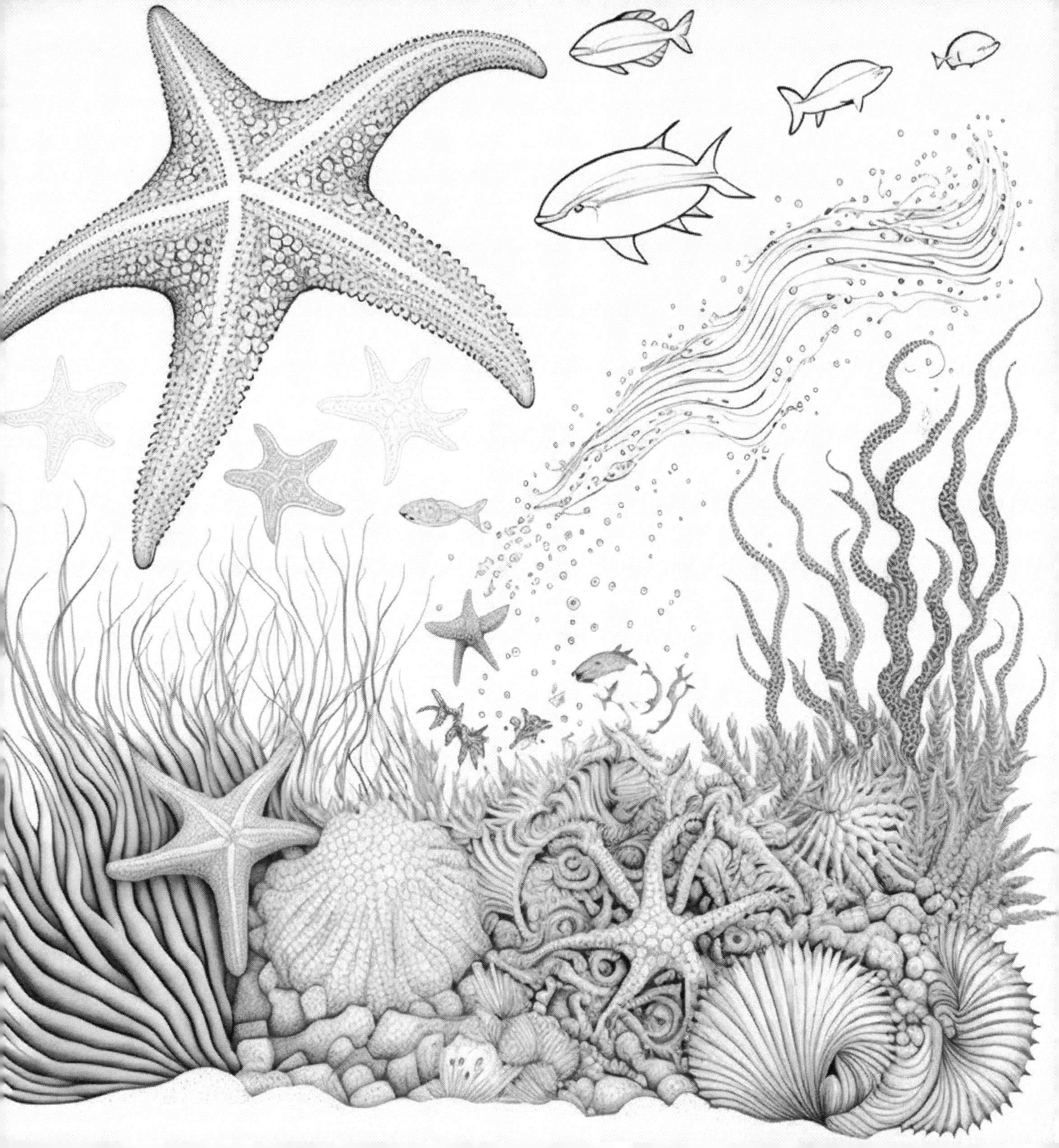

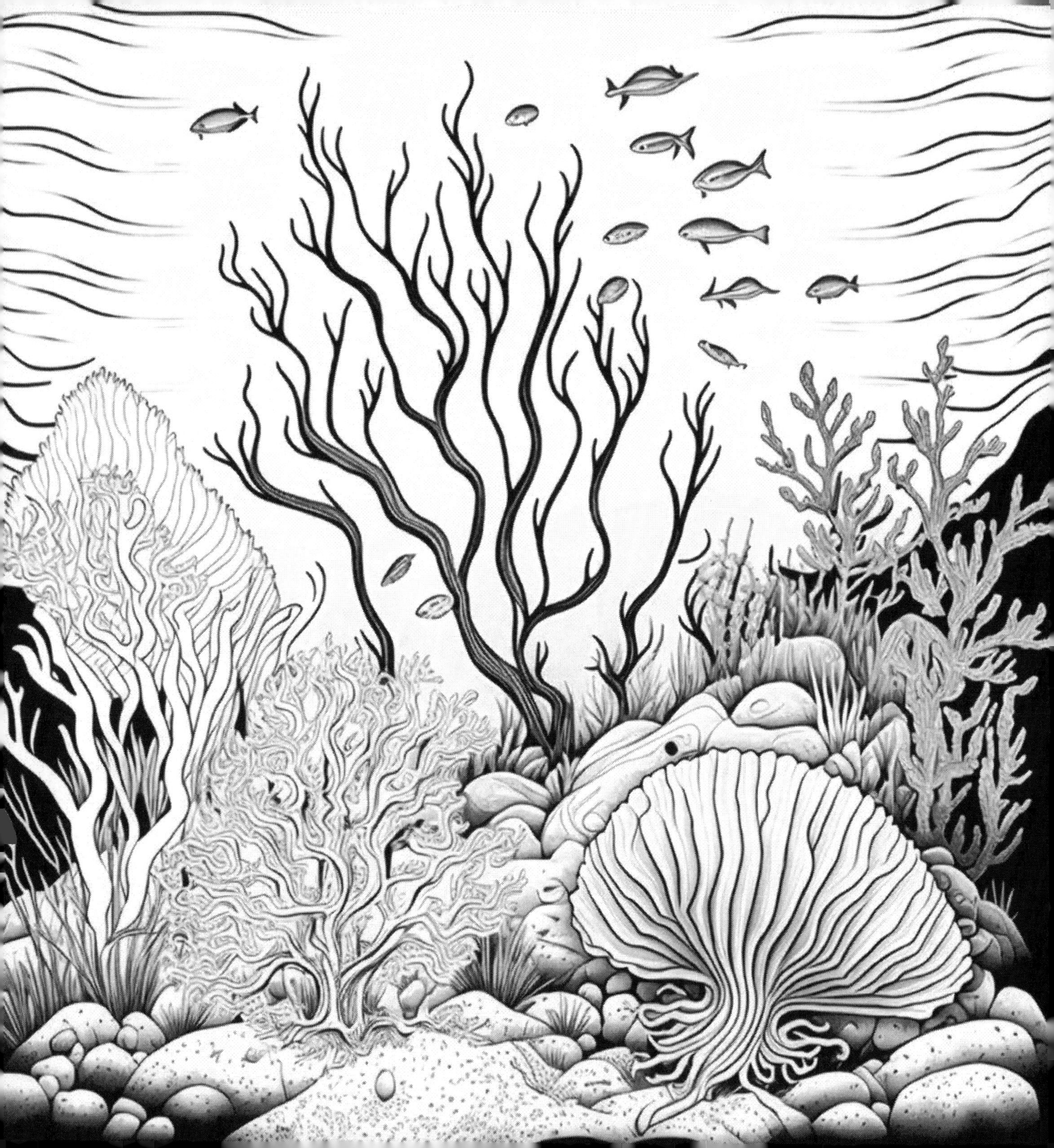

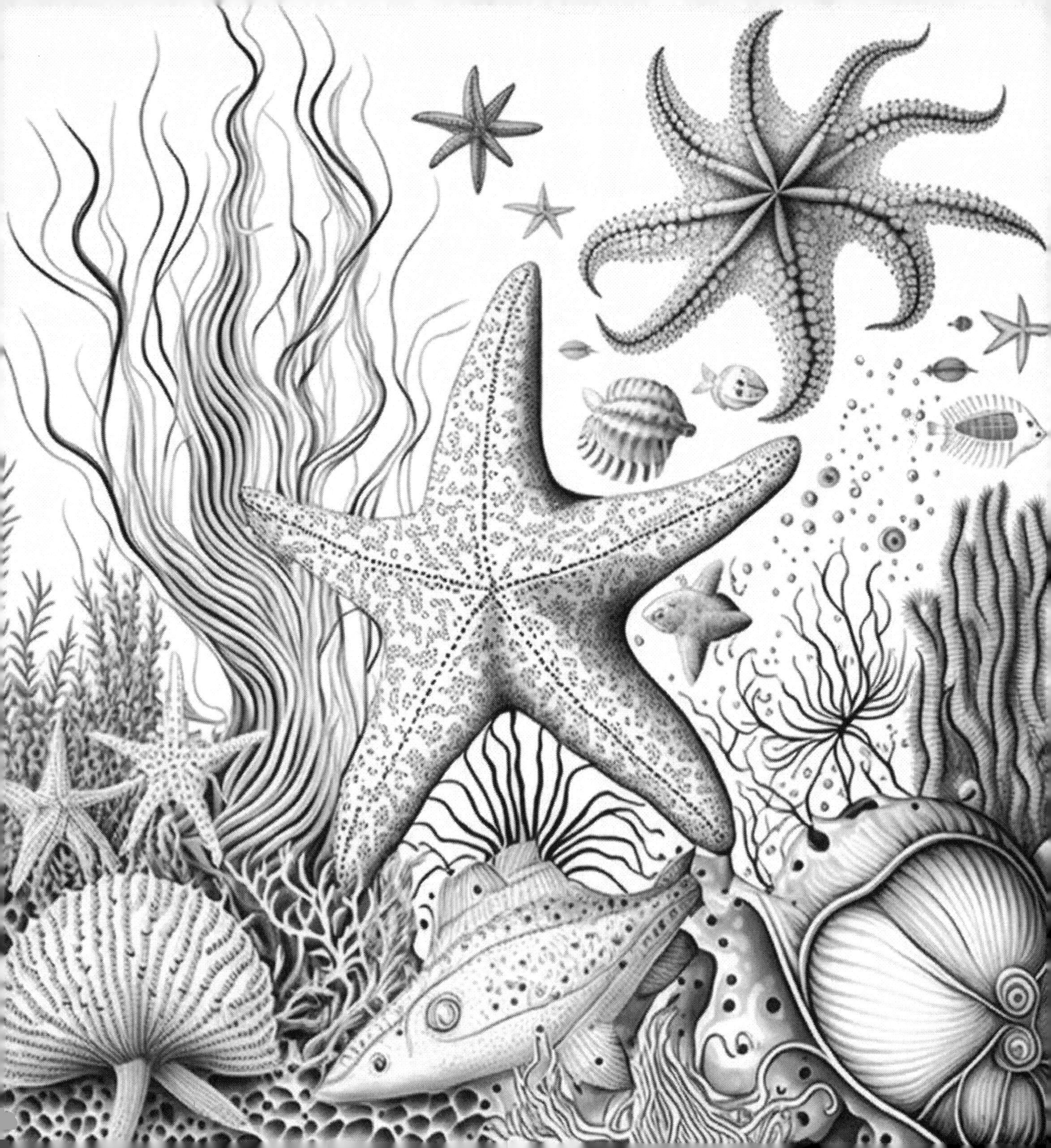

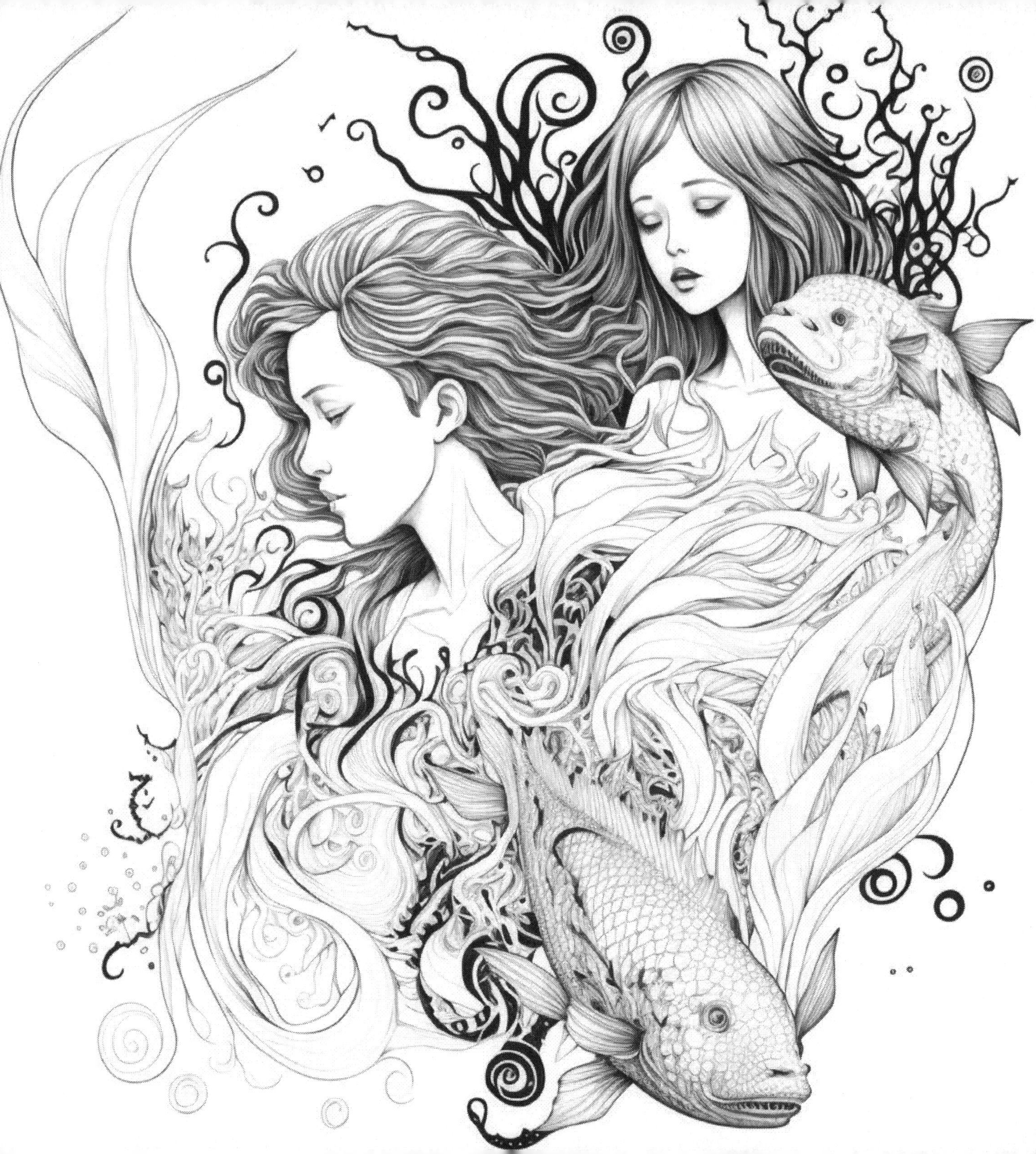

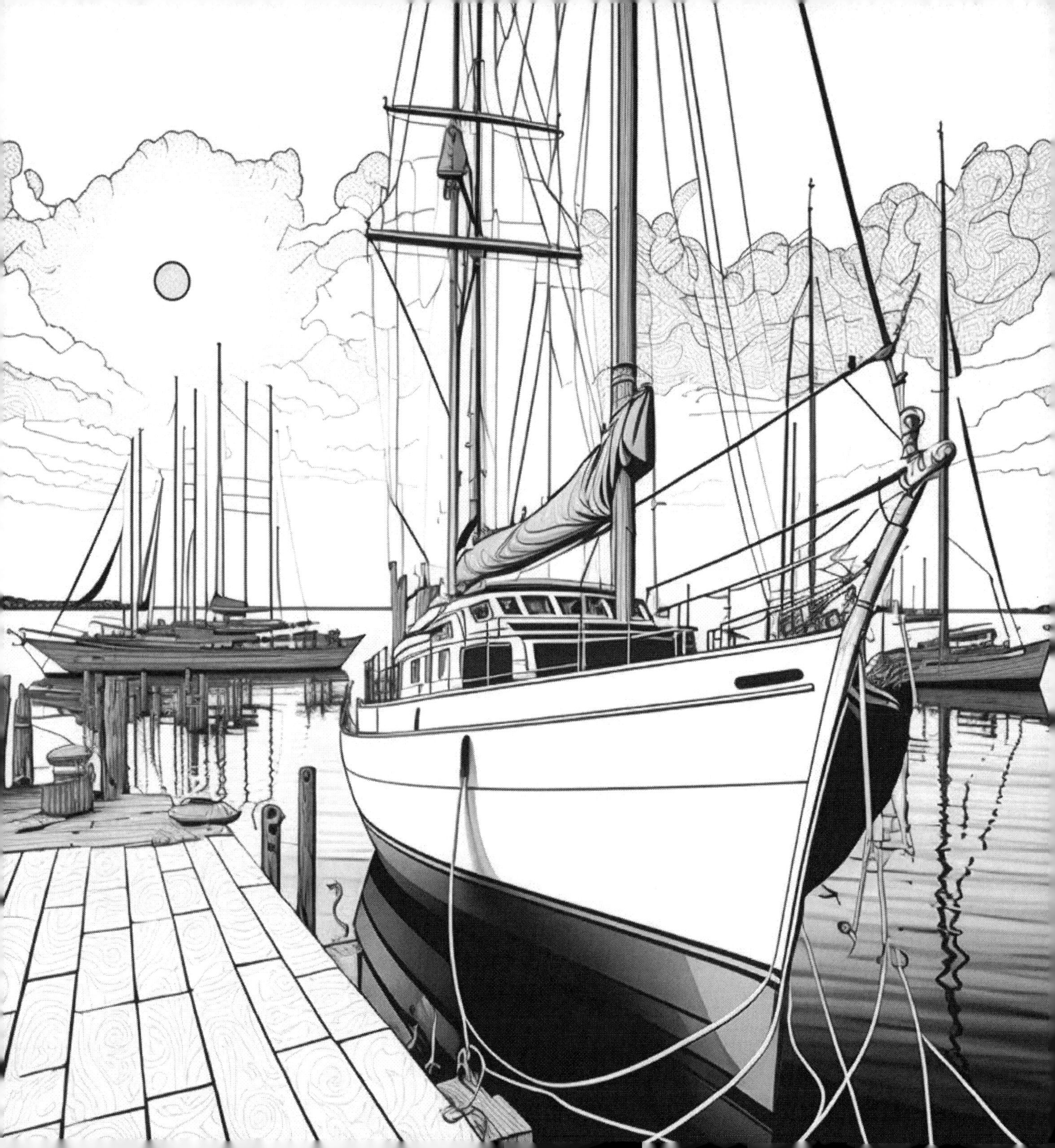

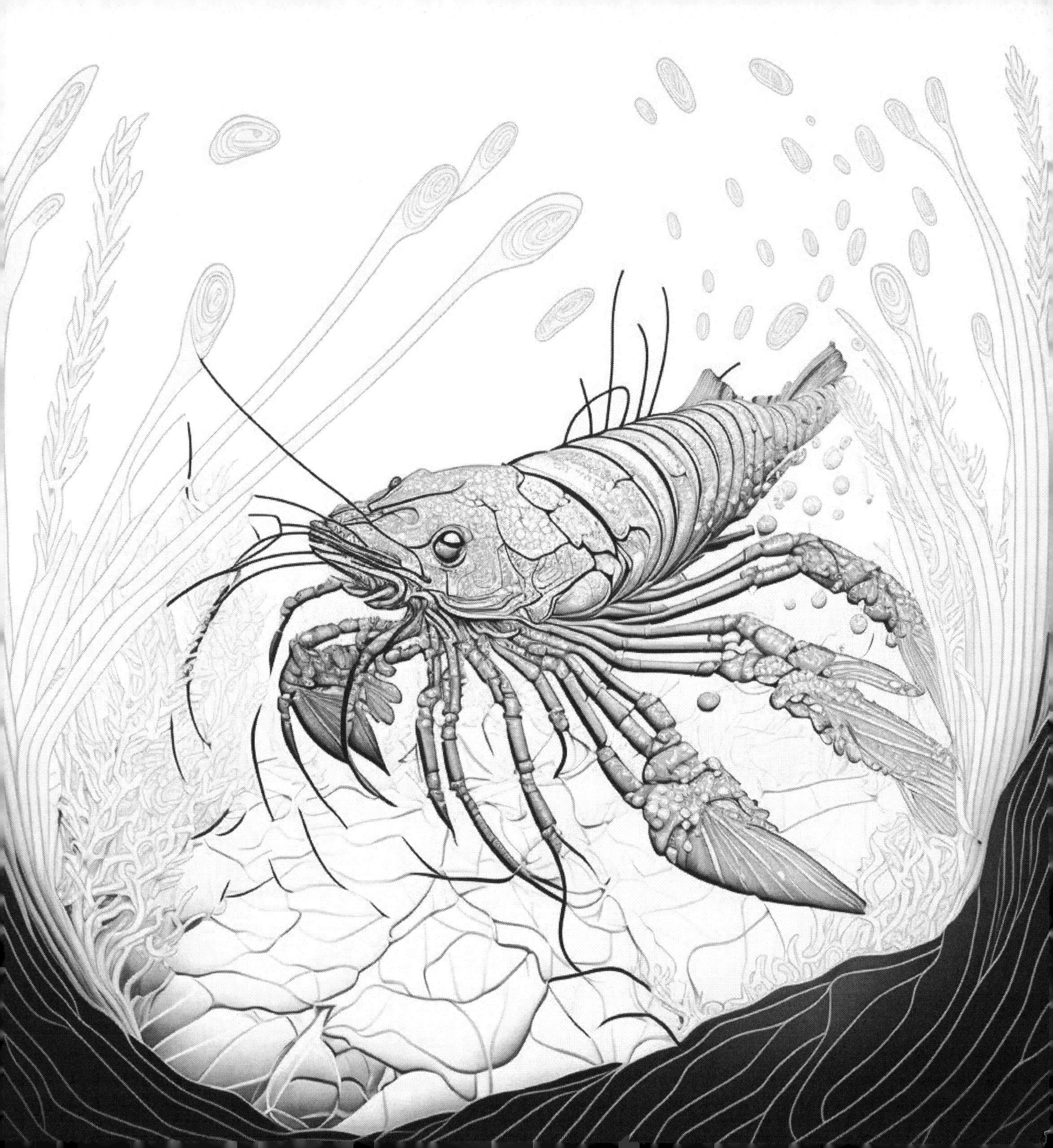

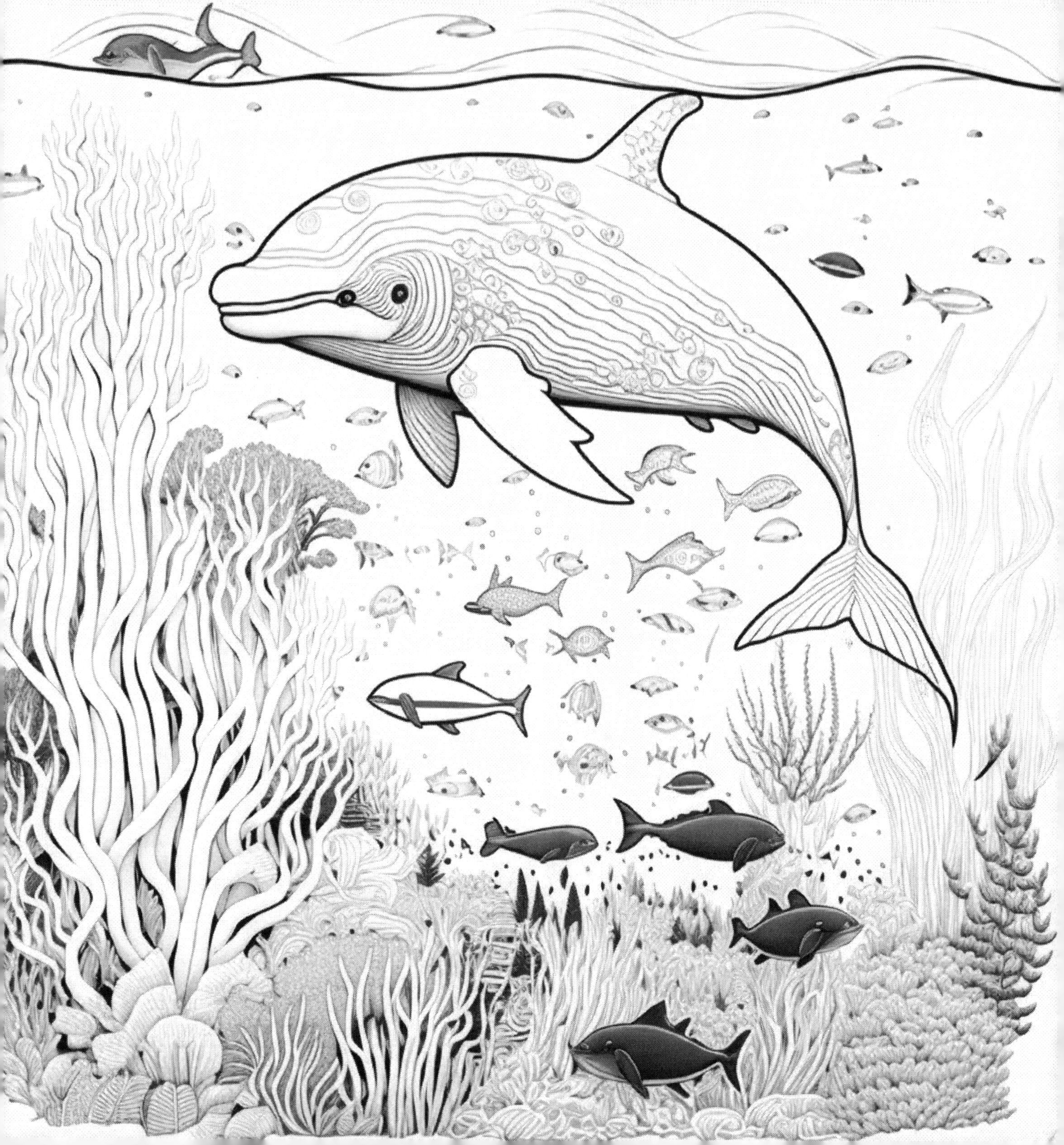

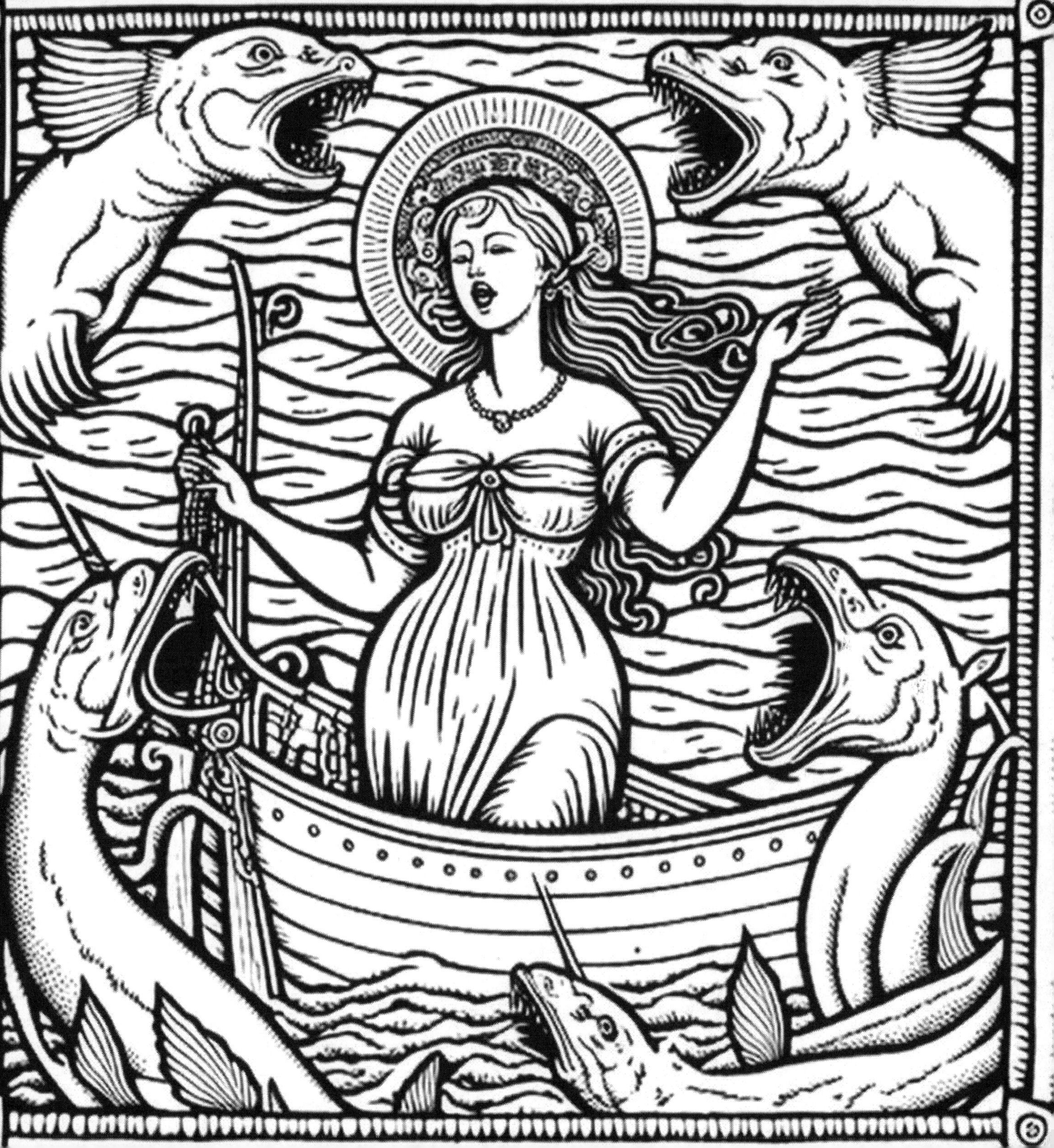

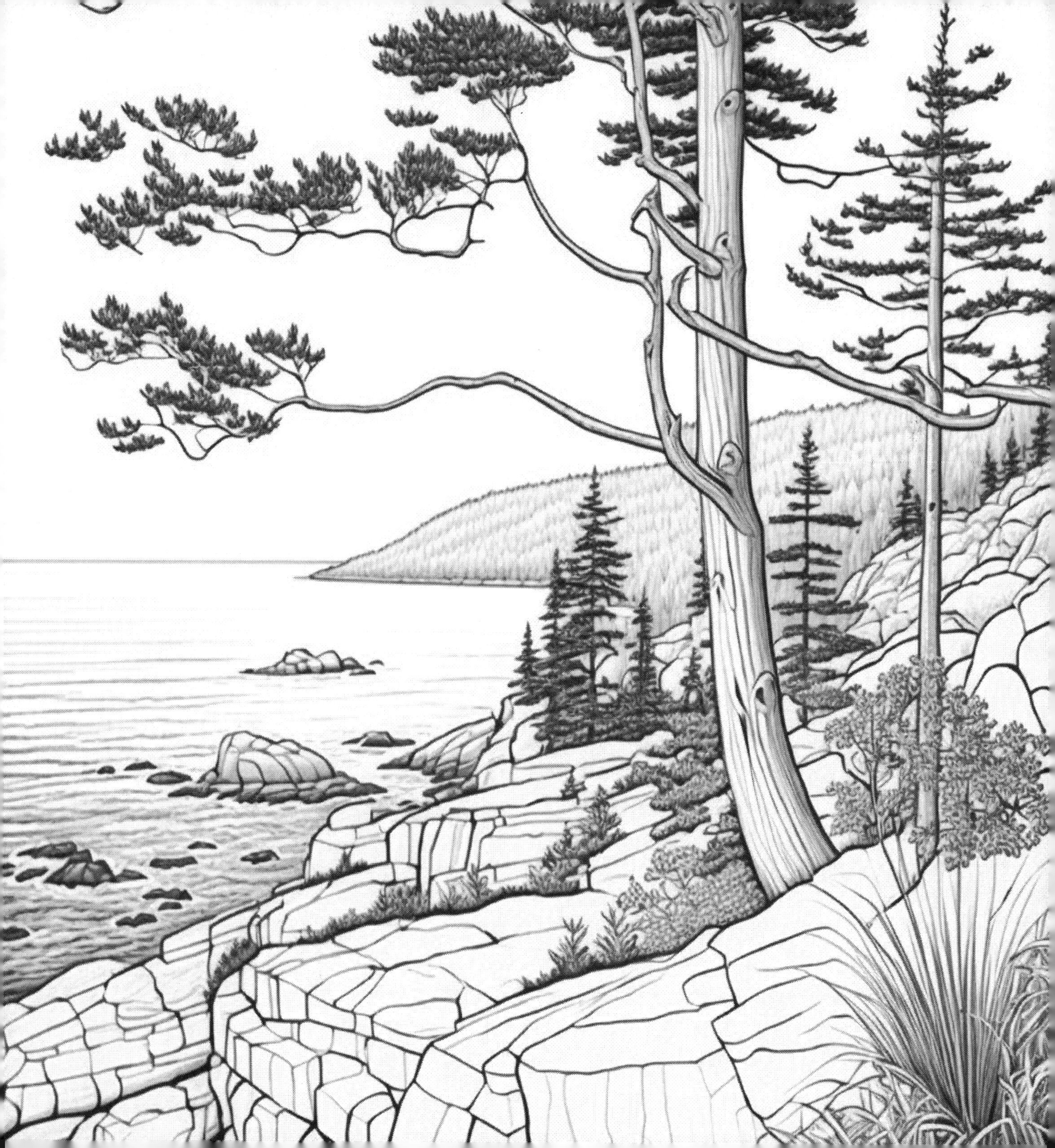

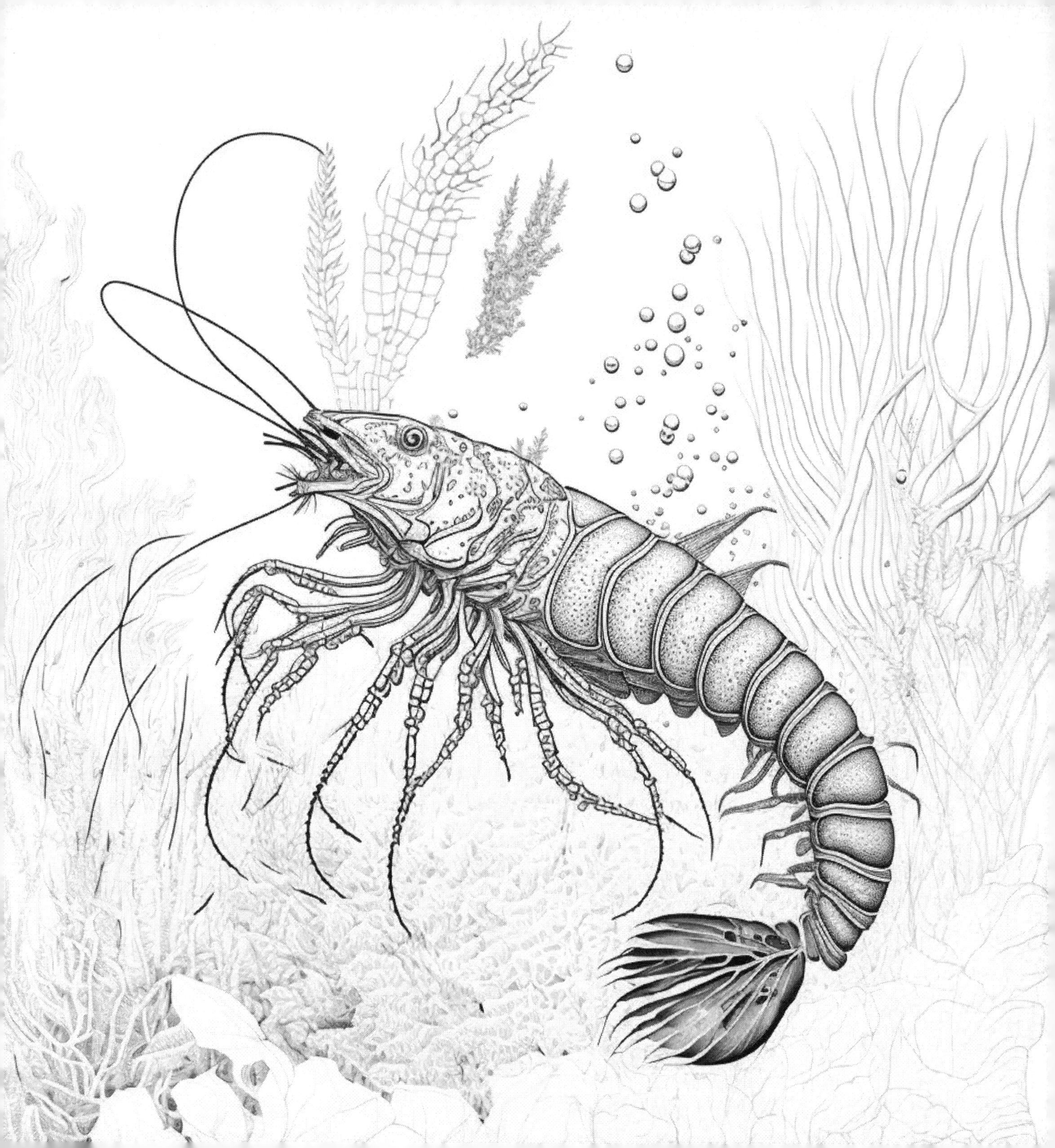

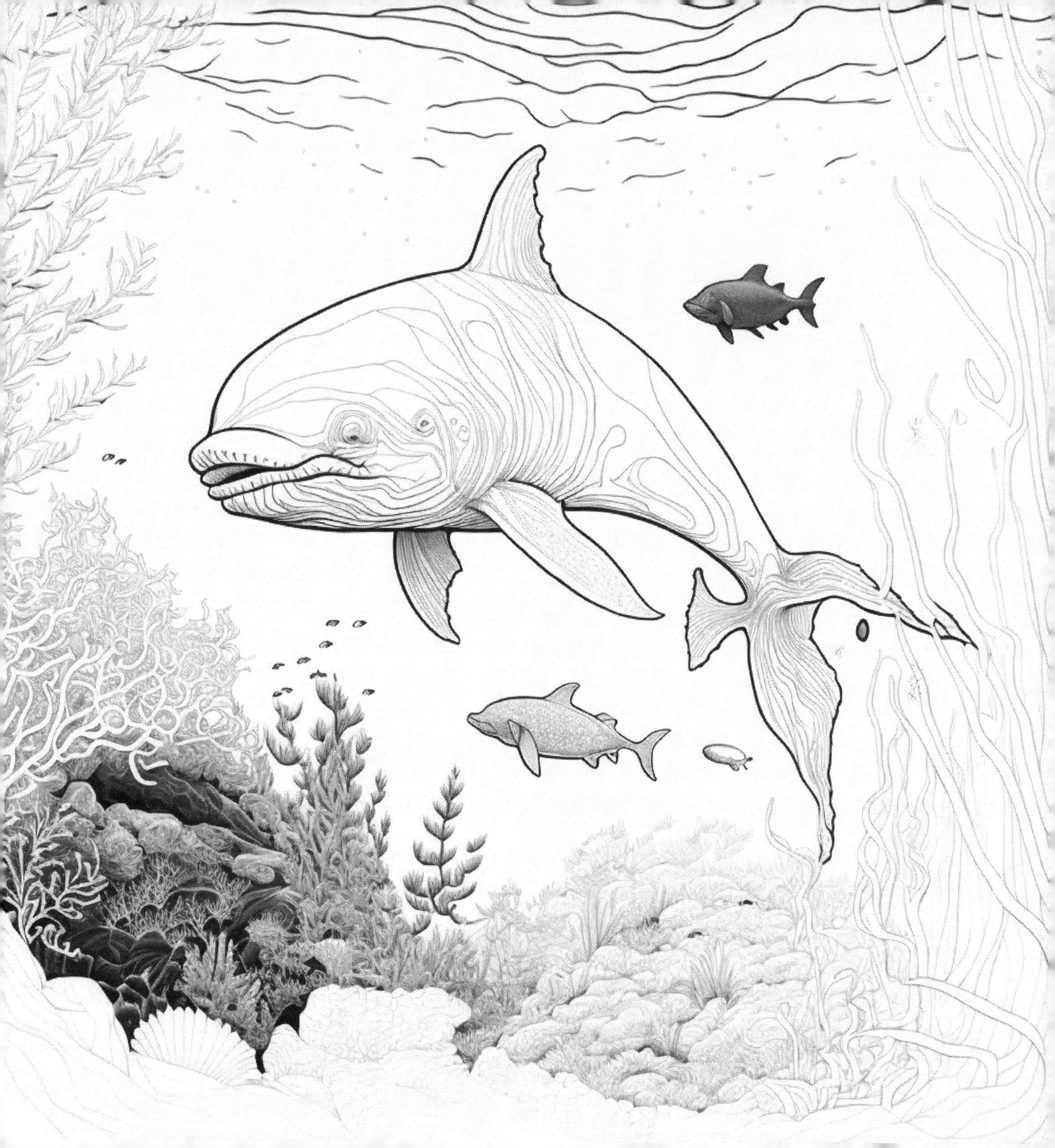

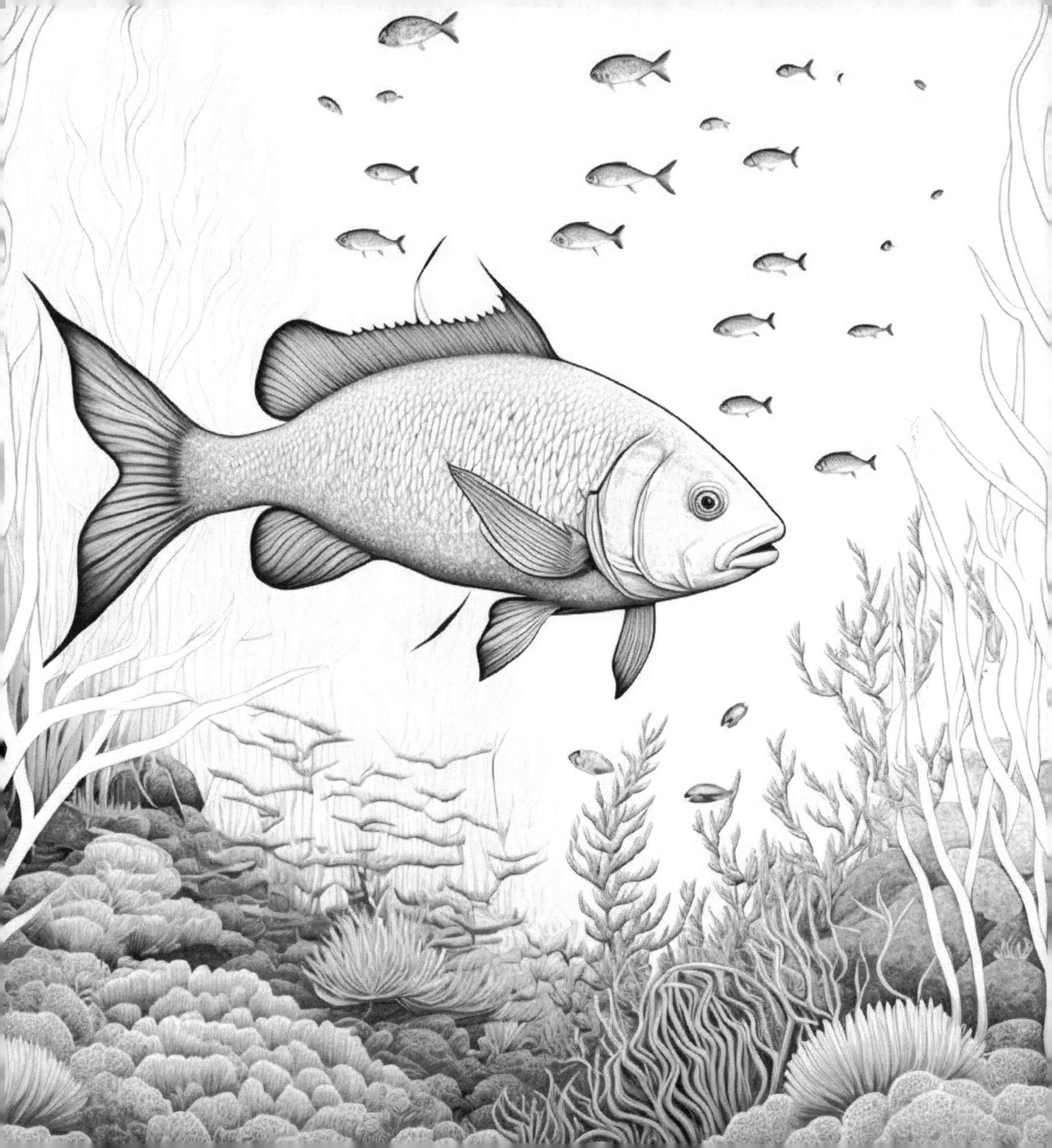

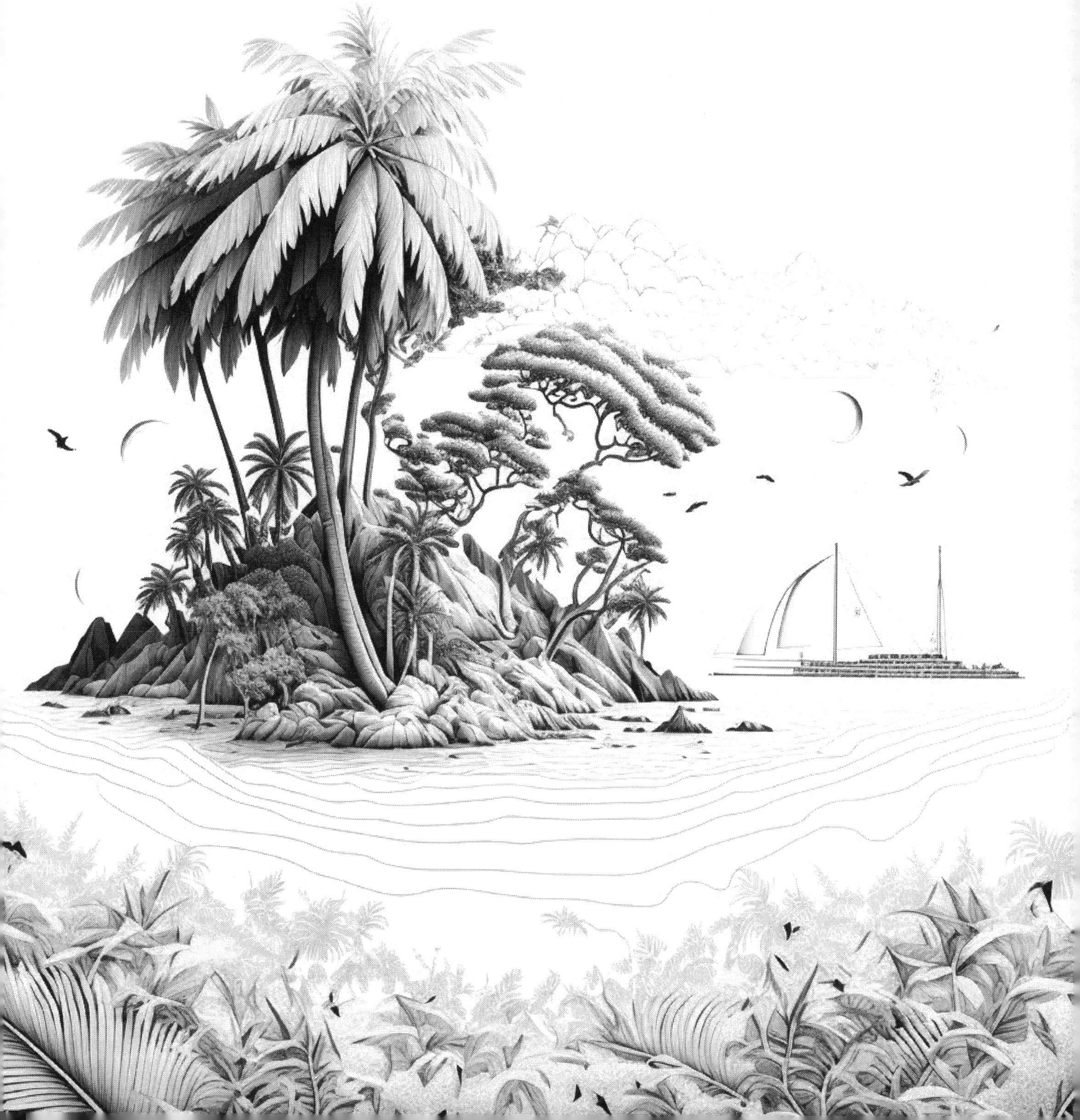

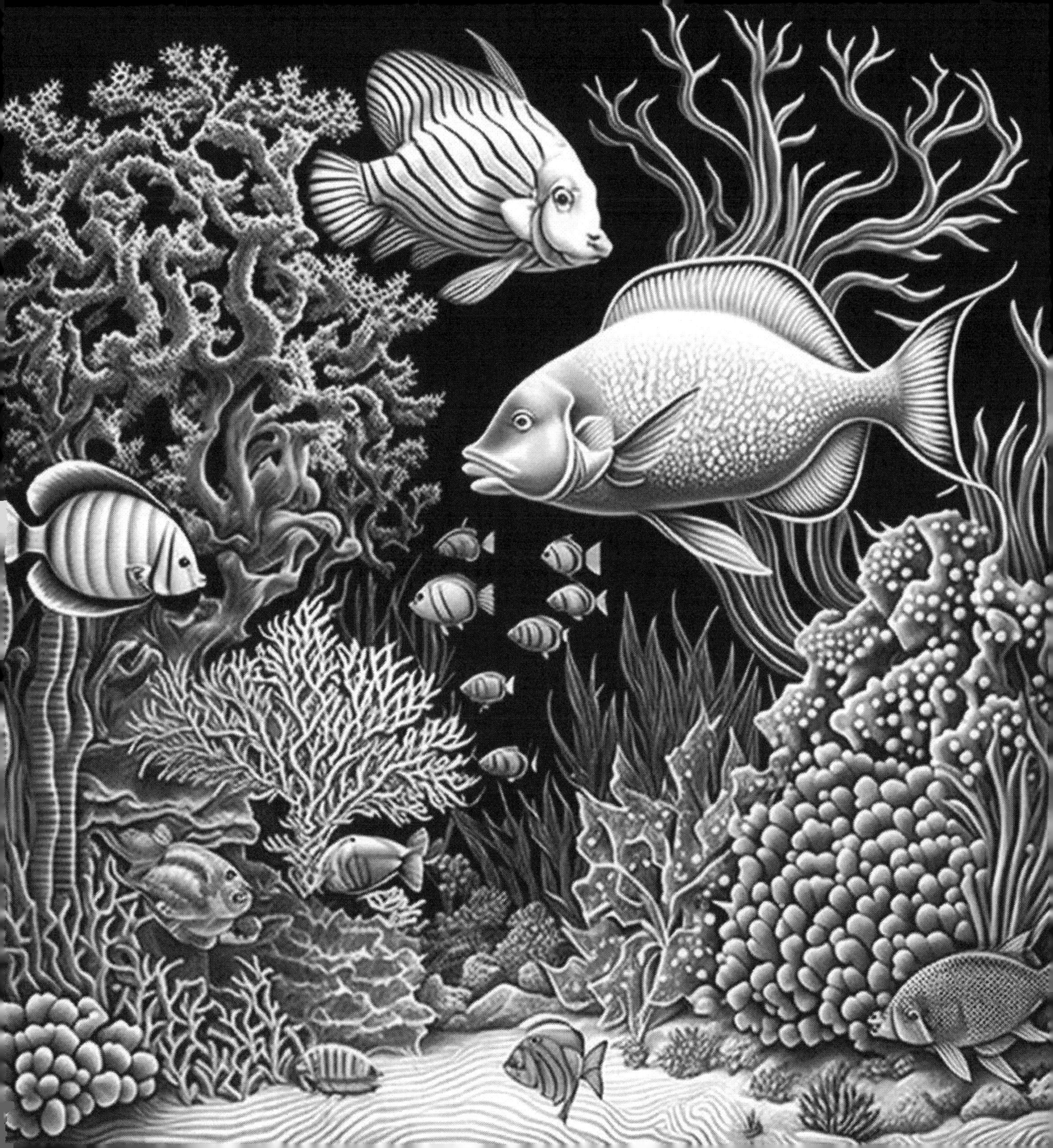

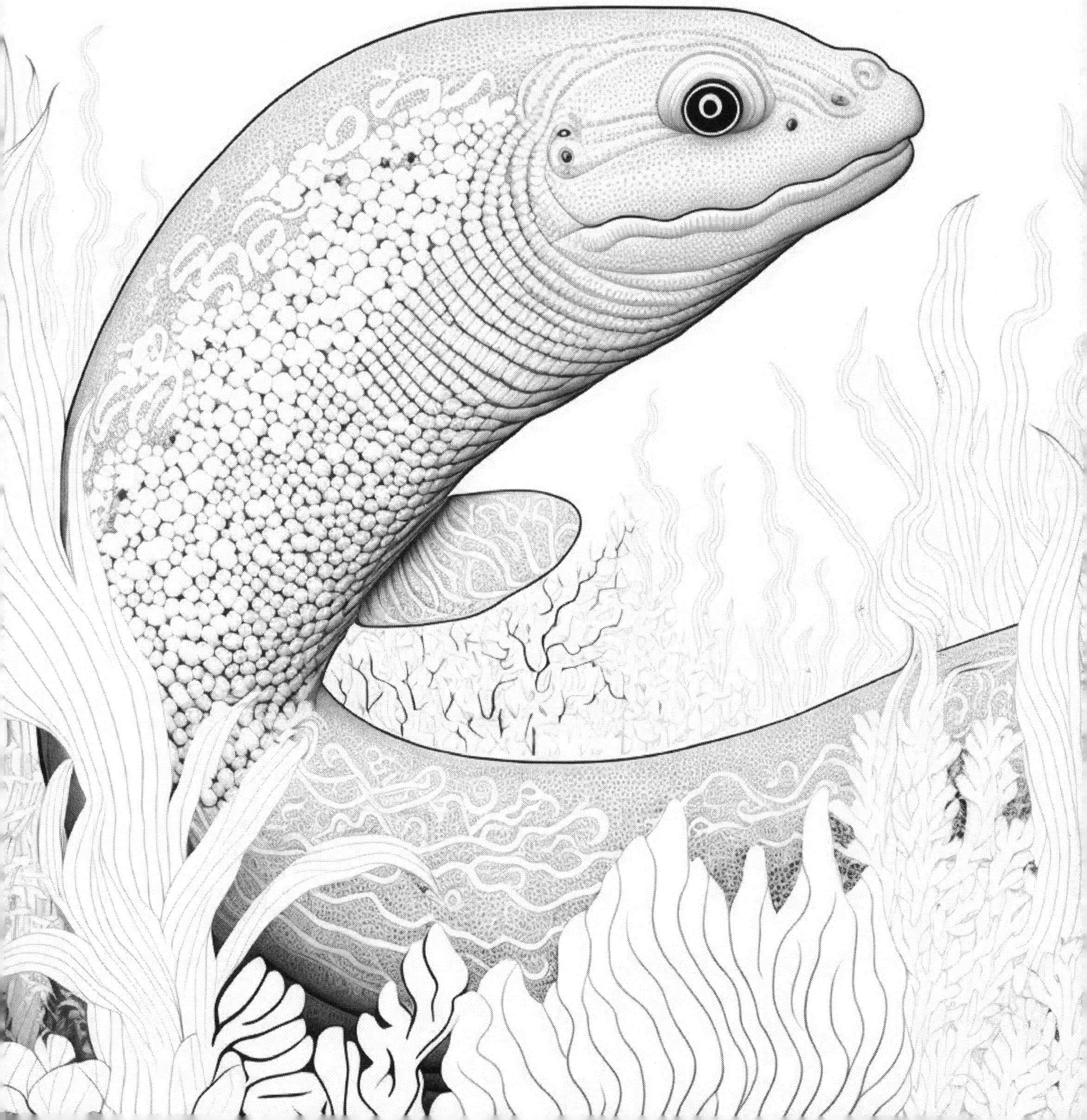

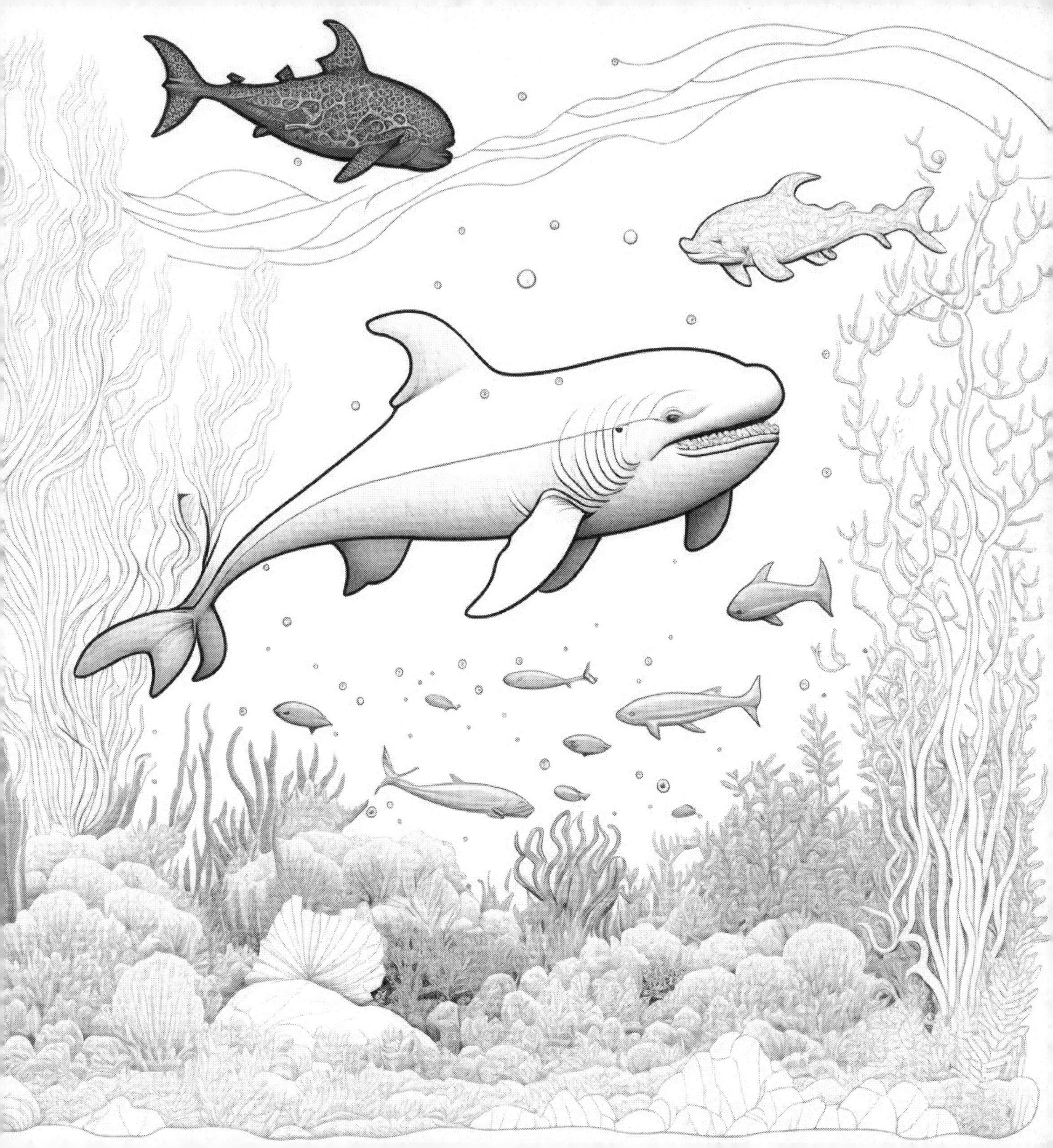

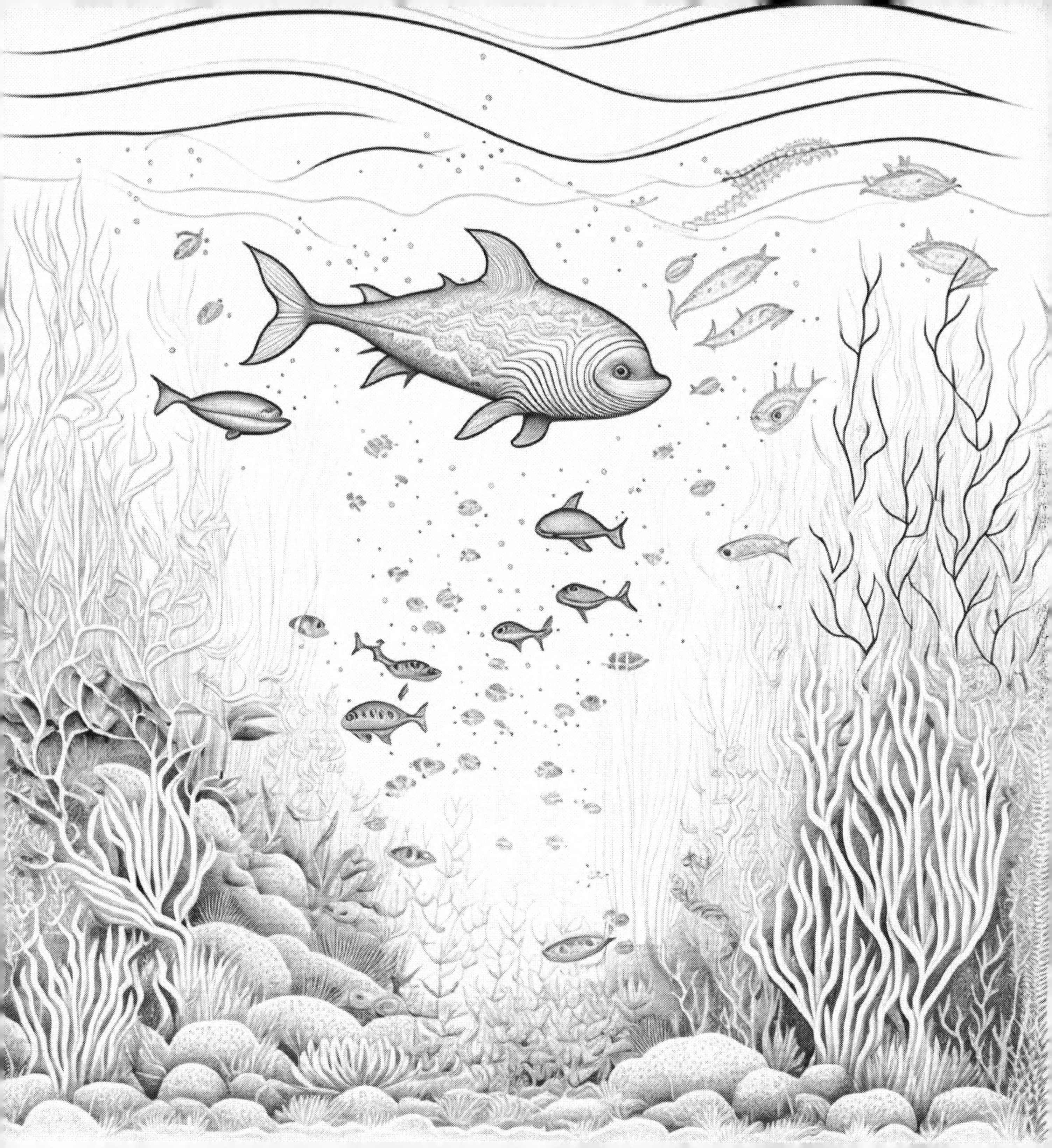

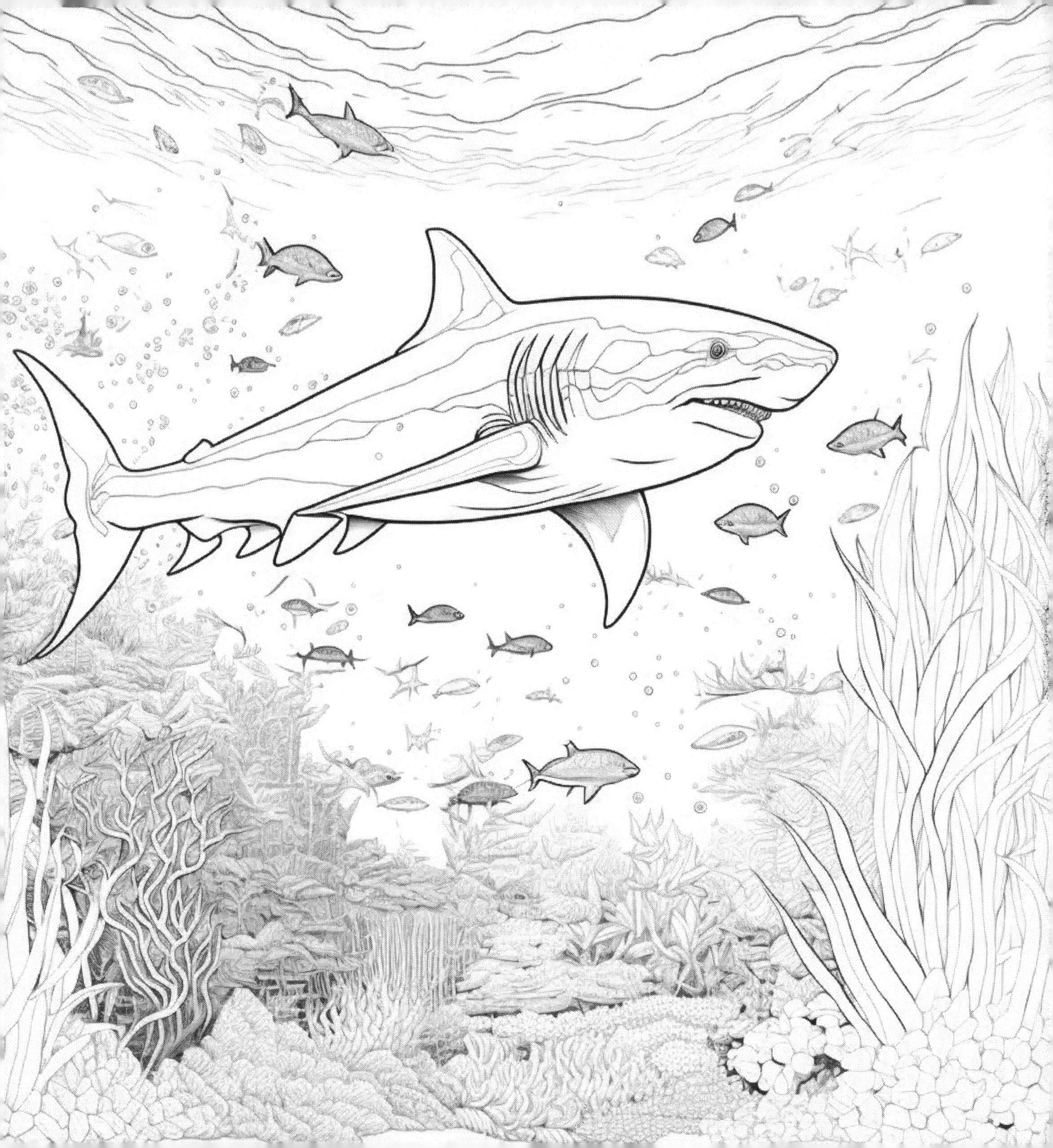

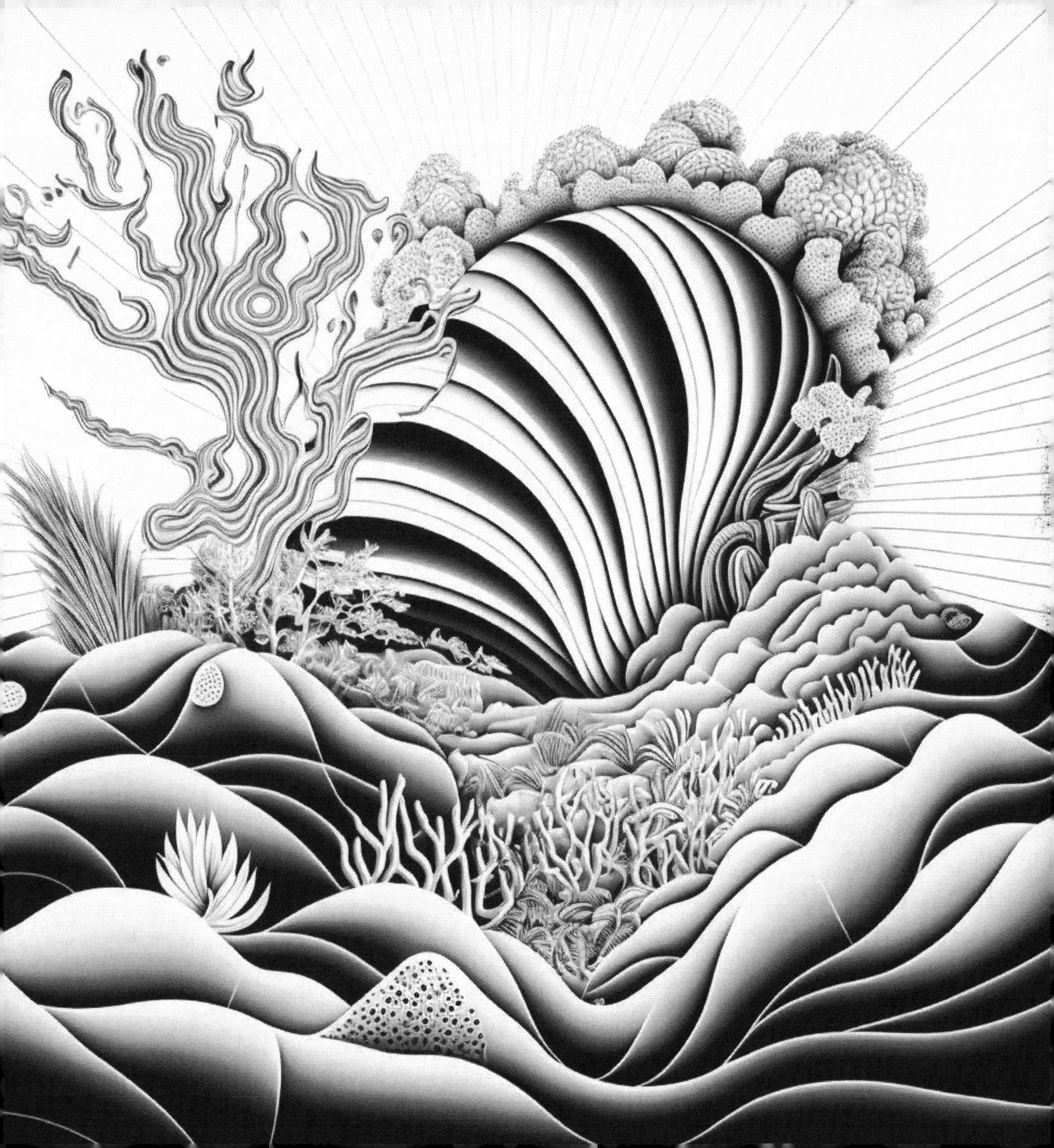

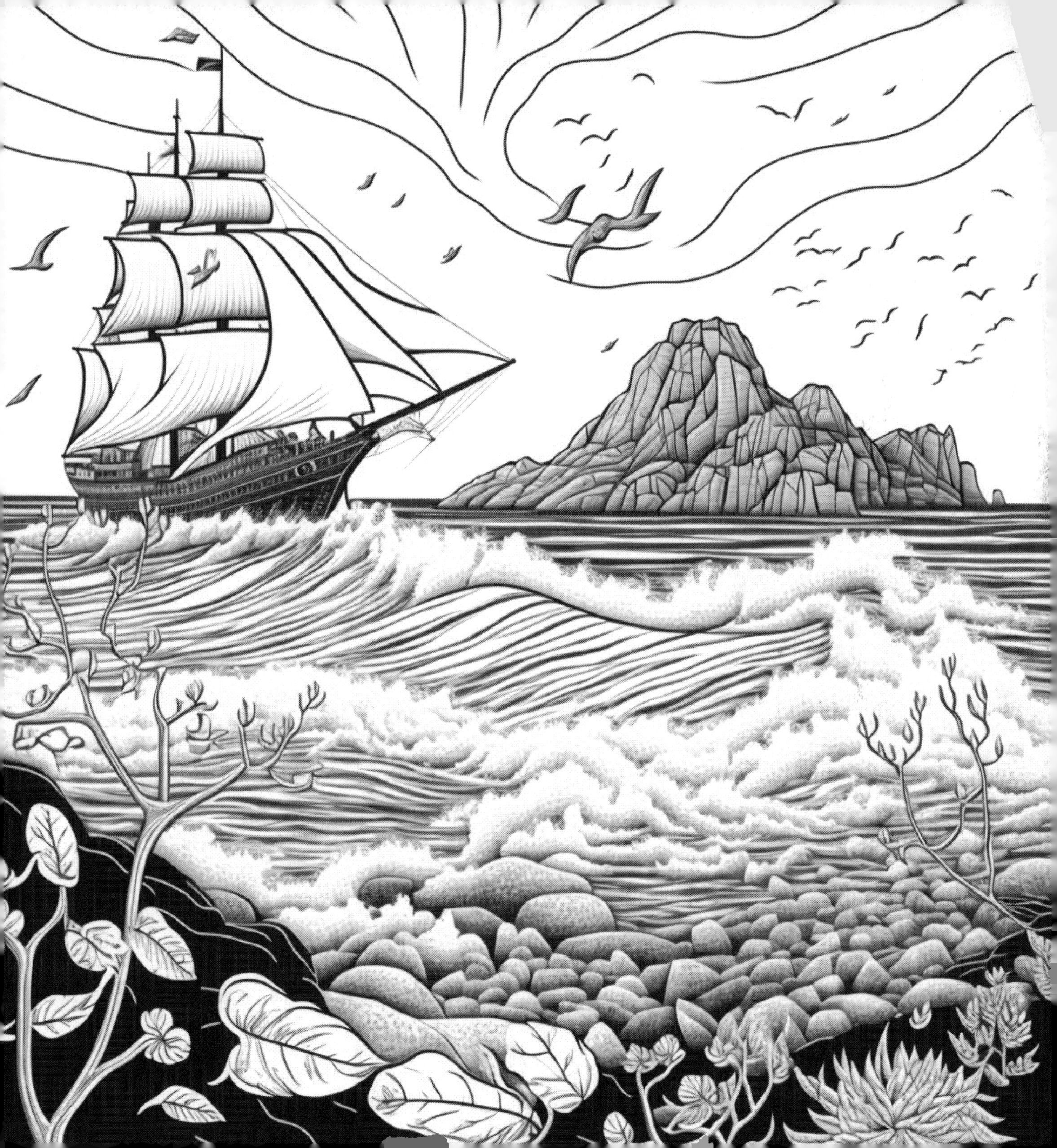

Made in United States
Orlando, FL
07 May 2023

32890601R00057